How to use VETERAN'S PREFERENCE To Get a GOVERNMENT JOB

Four-Star Tactics and Strategies for Active Military, Veterans, Spouses, Parents of Veterans

Glenn S. Millsaps, Jr., MBA

US Marine Corps Veteran

authorHOUSE®

AuthorHouse™ LLC
1663 Liberty Drive
Bloomington, IN 47403
www.authorhouse.com
Phone: 1-800-839-8640

Published by AuthorHouse   05/01/2014

ISBN: 978-1-4969-0736-3 (sc)
ISBN: 978-1-4969-0735-6 (hc)
ISBN: 978-1-4969-0734-9 (e)

Library of Congress Control Number: 2014908265

Dedication

This book is in honor of the enormous hard work, effort, and dedication of this nation's veterans who wish to continue their efforts by working for the government they defended.

"I'm not interested in changing history, but I
am interested in changing the future."

—Author Unknown

For my children Kelsey, Justice, Hope, Holly, and Glenn III, and William Barry McCain, Retired Navy, for helping me when I needed it most.

TABLE OF CONTENTS

FOREWORD

MEMORANDUM FOR CHIEF HUMAN CAPITAL OFFICERS[1]

From: **John Berry,** Director of the United States Office **of Personnel Management (OPM)**

Subject: **VOW (Veterans Opportunity to Work) to Hire Heroes Act of 2011**

On November 21, 2011, President Obama signed the VOW (Veterans Opportunity to Work) to Hire Heroes Act of 2011 (Public Law 112-56). The VOW Act amends chapter 21 of title 5, United States Code (U.S.C.) by adding section 2108a, "Treatment of certain individuals as veterans, disabled veterans, and preference eligible's." This new section requires Federal agencies to treat certain active duty service members as preference eligible's for purposes of an appointment in the competitive service, even though the service members have not been discharged or released from active duty.

Many members of the armed forces start their civilian job search prior to discharge or release from active duty and thus do not have a DD form 214 when applying for Federal jobs. The VOW Act was enacted to ensure these individuals do not lose the opportunity to be considered for Federal service (and awarded their veterans' preference entitlements if applicable) despite not having a DD form 214 to submit along with their résumés.

This new section requires Federal agencies to treat active duty service members as veterans and preference eligible's under section 2108 when they submit a "certification" when applying for a Federal job. The "certification"

---

[1]   http://www.chcoc.gov/transmittals/TransmittalDetails.aspx?TransmittalID=4881

is any written document from the armed forces that certifies the service member is expected to be discharged or released from active duty service in the armed forces under honorable conditions not later than 120 days after the date the certification is signed. Therefore, agencies must accept applications and consider for appointment and veterans' preference any service member who submits a certification in lieu of a DD form 214. Prior to appointment, agencies must verify the service member is eligible for veterans' preference in accordance with 5 U.S.C. 2108, unless the service member is appointed under the provisions of 5 U.S.C. 5534a, "Dual employment and pay during terminal leave from uniformed services."

The Office of Personnel Management is reviewing its regulations, guidance, web sites, etc., to ensure that the provisions of 5 U.S.C. 2108a are incorporated into these policy vehicles. We are attaching a Fact Sheet (Attachment A) and Frequently Asked Questions (Attachment B) on VOW for your information. These attachments will be posted on OPM's website. If you have any questions, please feel free to contact Michael J. Mahoney, Manager, Hiring Policy, at mike.mahoney@opm.gov or at 202-606-1142.

PREFACE

"A federal employee, who is a veteran, may apply to a
higher pay grade level under the VRA, and we must keep
all applications for at least one year after an announcement
has closed."

—Federal Human Resources Specialist

HOW TO USE THIS GUIDE

This book is mainly about how veterans can best use their veteran's
preference rights for employment purposes. I have read other books about
the laws that protect veterans, but they do not go into any detail about
the application process of those rights as they apply to resumes and where
your name may appear on a certificate of eligible. Most veterans do not
know how a certificate of eligible applies to veteran's preference. Imagine
if you had an upper hand in getting hired with a respected employer. You
do—and with no handouts! As a veteran, regardless of your challenges, you
have earned the right to claim veteran's preference on federal applications,
including some state and local jobs. Most state and local governments do
not have extensive policy guidelines compared to the federal government
on veteran preference rights. No other special group in our population
has a hiring preference except for Native Americans. Regardless of your
national origin, race, color, or creed, your veteran's preference rights are
all intact. The use of this book depends on how you want to use it. There
are no conventions to this guide. From what I can tell, most of the case
law presented in this guide begins to run in a circle. No individual case
is better than another, but you do want to find case law that is on point
if you find yourself needing to protect your preference eligibility rights.
The circle is one veteran's preference right violation after another. As you
read through this guide, you will begin to notice degrees of nuances.

These degrees of nuances are very difficult to pick up on, and there are thousands—if not millions—of them. For instance, many selecting officials make job announcements and list several certificates of eligibles under one job announcement. Under this scenario, like almost every veteran's preference right violation, the selecting official unlawfully fails to make a passover procedure of a qualified veteran. Passover procedures require federal agencies to notify the US Office of Personnel Management that they are requesting to select a nonveteran under applicable law. It is up to the preference-eligible applicant to stop this from occurring. During my career, I have investigated thousands of complaints, and you would not believe how many veterans' preference violations I have encountered. Many of them go unaddressed because the veteran did not follow up on the status of an application. Veteran's preference violations occur with great frequency.

ACKNOWLEDGMENTS

"Maintain your stamina and hold, or you will be damaged."
—Author Unknown

Thank you to all the people who took the time to read through this book. Thank you to everyone who has served. To retired US EEOC Investigator John Treadwell, my mentor, friend, and partner in crime. To the Maricopa County NAACP President Rev. Oscar Tillman for all the support you have been over the many years. He has been an awesome go-to man. To retired US Marine Corps Sergeant Major Herman Raybon for your protection and being a real Marine leader and taking good care of your people. To Tim Colvin, my best friend, for being almost the first-to-last person to inspire me to join the United States Marine Corps, for letting me stay with you when I left home at sixteen, for remembering our strong friendship of twenty-plus years despite our different directions, and raising good kids as a single father. Tim, despite the fact you joined the Army, I still love you man! To Coach Dale Fox, for all the long talks and rides home from wrestling practice. To every person who intentionally put diversity in my path. I sincerely thank you from the bottom of my Marine Corps heart. To my mother who taught me long ago that a bird can only fly high for so long before it has to come down for water. My mom is the wisest, meanest, loveliest, sincerest, and most intelligent person I know. Why do I say this? My mom, who has no knowledge of military life, once told a Navy chaplain these words, "You can lead a horse to water, but you can't make it drink. You should do everything you can do to see that my son comes home to his grandfather's funeral." To my dad, for being silent when it was time. To my beloved grandfather, for *everything* he stood for. To all my uncles on my dad's side of the family for being men of candor and great strength, especially to my Uncle Leonard (Navy) and his dear wife, for showing me there is more to life than my home town and letting me stay for the summer with them in New York. To my Uncle Jerry (Army) for looking like the meanest but really being very humble. To my Uncle Rudolf (Duck) for being my uncle but inspiring me with his fatherlike qualities. To my Uncle Baxter (Army) for being humble through his life despite diversity. To Kelly Summers for teaching me to gracefully handle relationships. To my Aunt Edith for keeping my siblings and me when my mom got sick. To my cousins Marvin, Melvin, and Jermal (from New York) for all you taught me and my brother Kevin. I talk about you guys a lot. To all the members of my home church (Zion Chapel) for making sure I left home with a Bible. To all my Marine Corps drill instructors for teaching me honor, courage, and commitment.

I thank *you all*, plus many others. All of you have added a sense of meaning and quality to my life. Whoever says it doesn't take a village to raise a kid is wrong.

Now for whom I really want to thank: Jesus Christ. Thank you so much. I could not do what I believe in without you in my life.

AUTHOR'S NOTE

This book is not free. A great deal of time, energy, and research were spent putting this book together. I am asking each person who has decided to purchase a copy to please not pass it on to others. If you find other veterans who need this information, help them purchase a copy. Tell others about this book: I do not want one more day to go by with another veteran homeless or jobless because he or she did not have the right knowledge. I have personally visited many homeless shelters and found many veterans who are jobless because they lack the information I've included in this book. I have been able to assist many on a one-on-one basis, but this book can cover more ground in this hopeful mission. What I have outlined in this book works. I have arranged to donate many of this book's proceeds to paralyzed veterans and wounded warriors. Your purchase will help me to continue to volunteer my time to the many veterans in need.

Sincerely & Semper Fi.
Glenn S. Millsaps Jr.

Glossary of Terms

Below are the designated veteran's preference codes you will see on a certificate of eligibility list. They are the categories of veteran's preference codes to which a veteran applicant is entitled:

CPS Ten-point 30 percent compensable disability preference based on a service-connected disability of 30 percent or more.

CP Ten-point compensable disability preference based on a service-connected disability of 10 percent or more, but less than 30 percent.

XP Ten-point disability preference. Granted to recipients of the Purple Heart and persons with a noncompensable service-connected disability (less than 10 percent).

XP Ten percent derived preference. Granted to widow or widower or mother of a deceased veteran or a spouse or mother of a disabled veteran. (Note that the father of a veteran does not qualify for "granted" preference.)

TP Five-point preference.

NV Designates a nonveteran. (This is an optional code that delegated examining offices may use. A blank space is also used to designate nonveterans.)

Delegated examining office: A human resource office of a federal agency that has been delegated human resource functions by the US Office of Personnel Management.

Certificate of eligibles: This is a list of applicants who were found to be qualified. There can be many certificates of eligibles issued under one job announcement by a federal agency (i.e., Veterans Employment

Opportunity Act (VEOA) list, transfer list, Veterans Recruitment Act (VRA) list, Schedule A list).

Freedom of Information Act: This act allows for the full or partial disclosure of previously unreleased information and documents controlled by the US government. The act explicitly applies to only executive branch government agencies. Executive branches are the federal agencies to which you will be applying.

DELEGATED EXAMINING OPERATIONS HANDBOOK (DEOH): The manual written by the Office of Personnel Management. This handbook is the guide passed down to all federal agencies.

US OFFICE OF PERSONNEL MANAGEMENT (OPM): This office controls the human resources functions of most, if not all, federal agencies. OPM has delegated its human resource function to other federal agencies.

WWW.USAJOBS.GOV: The official federal government site where veterans and civilians apply for jobs listed by federal agencies.

SELECTING OFFICIAL: The person assigned by an agency to hire a qualified applicant.

MERIT SYSTEM PROTECTION BOARD: The MSPB is an independent quasi-judicial agency that protects employees under the federal merit system against partisan and other prohibited personnel practices. MSPB has jurisdiction over a veteran preference violation.

OCCUPATIONAL SERIES: A listing of federal government occupations.

Title VII: Title VII of the Civil Rights Act of 1964 protects individuals against employment discrimination on the bases of race, color, national origin, sex, and religion. It also applies to employment agencies and labor organizations, as well as to the federal government.

Notice of result: Notification from the examining office giving applicants notice of whether they were found qualified and whether they referred for consideration. (This notice starts the clock of time limitations that apply to preference rights to request reconsideration or to file a complaint with the US Department of Labor.)

Understanding Veteran's Preference Rights

"The day the soldiers stop bringing you their problems is the day you stopped leading them. They have either lost confidence that you can help them or concluded that you do not care. Either case is a failure of leadership."

—Colin Powell

Special Note to Parents of Veterans

I wanted to talk to the special people who send their young men and women to serve in the armed forces in a way I wish someone could have spoken to my parents when I decided to served. Many parents (particularly mothers) of the young servicemen and servicewomen are unaware that they too are preference-eligible under limited circumstances. This eligibility depends on the disability rating of the child in the event he or she is injured while serving. I believe it is important to stay involved in the life of your child while he or she is serving. In many ways, the armed forces are similar to the job market. My suggestion is that each time your child goes on sick call, you ask your child to request a copy and send it to you. Maintain these copies in a special location in the event your child is discharged for medical reasons. After all, the military does misplace files. On another note, talk to your service member and encourage him or her to get an education while in the service. Many young servicemen and servicewomen spend their time partying like rock stars and find that it is difficult to get serious about the job market after their tours of duty. Many young service members do not really understand the civilian job market. They will articulate their knowledge, skills, and ability to potential employers, but they should have done volunteer work, enrolled in college level courses, and kept track of supervisors and managers who could one day provide letters of recommendation.

Veterans Are Not Told

In 1994, I passed the military entrance exam (ASVAB) and was then shipped to Parris Island, South Carolina, in a twelve-passenger van. I thus began my journey to becoming a United States Marine. At best, it was an intimidating experience. Once I arrived on the island and got out of that van, a drill instructor who stood about 6'5" (at least he seemed) came out of a dark building wearing a Smokey Bear cover, unpleasant as a pit of pissed off rattle snakes, and began demanding that we move it, move it, move it, *you* damn maggots, get off *my* bus and put your little nasty toes on those yellow footprints. I was senseless enough to wonder what we did wrong. I thought *Full Metal Jacket* was just a movie. Nonetheless, many of us did not know what civilian benefits were ahead of us. I sure do wish I could take back those days and find a book like the one you are about to read. We did have a foggy idea of the trouble ahead of us in the next thirteen weeks, though. Many veterans have a similarly foggy vision of veteran's preference rights and how they can benefit them.

DRAWBACKS TO VETERAN'S PREFERENCE RIGHTS

The good news is that most veteran's preference rights violations made by selecting officials in federal government are not made by veterans.

The bad news entails a drawback you might want to avoid. I'll use an example of a case I recently encountered. On about December 1, 2012, a female veteran who was honorably discharged after twenty years of active duty service applied for a job with a federal agency. She had already been employed by the federal agency when she submitted her application for a position the agency announced to all US citizens. The veteran was in a position that was a lower pay grade than the position she was seeking. The veteran hired into the federal government as a GS-5 and was seeking another position as a GS-11. Keep in mind the Veterans Recruitment Act permits a selecting official to hire a veteran into a position up to the GS-11 pay grade noncompetitively. When the veteran did not receive an interview and was subsequently not selected for the position, the veteran filed a complaint with the U S Department of Labor for veteran's preference rights (VEOA) violations. The Department of Labor found in the veteran's favor. When the agency did not comply with the Department of Labor's request to fix the veteran's preference claim violation, the veteran then filed a complaint with the US Merit System Protection Board. The board dismissed the complaint for lack of jurisdiction.

Here is the problem you may face under your preference eligibility rights: In the example mentioned above the board stated, "Under Title 5 CFR Section 302, an employee is not eligible to 'jump' from one pay grade to the next without first serving fifty-two weeks at the next lower pay grade." Regular pay grade increases usually go from GS-5 to GS-13 if the promotion potential is that high. In other words, no employee can move from GS-5 to GS-9 without doing a minimum of fifty-two weeks at the GS-7 grade level. Under the Veterans Recruitment Act (VRA), a veteran may be appointed to a grade level up to GS-11 if a selecting official chooses to have a heart. The danger of the VRA is that many selecting officials do not reach out to veterans and use the VRA certificate of eligible list. The exact reasons are unknown. The example I gave above was related to disability discrimination, which seems to be a common theme of the problems many veterans experience. I am strongly suggesting and pushing for a more consistent policy of VRA use with selections. You can help by contacting your Congressional representatives and asking them to get involved on this issue. Simply write or visit your representative and ask him or her to review the VRA and how agencies are using it. The VRA really has no effect because selecting officials may use it at their discretion. It is like having a criminal law in effect that allows prosecutors to act at their discretion in its enforcement.

Strengths and Limitations of This Book

This book gives you the knowledge you will need to understand why you may not get hired by the federal government. It is the only guide available to help you understand how to really navigate your veteran's preference rights through the federal system. The information I have provided here is a step in the right direction when researching jobs at www.usajobs.gov. No matter how much research I could have done for this book, the possibilities of games that are played are endless. There are so many different ways a federal agency can hire its staff, but your veteran's preference rights limit any unlawful activity. It is up to you to stop these violations from occurring. This book helps you limit some of your confusion.

My Assumptions of Your Knowledge

- I assumed you don't know how to get beyond the red tape you will face in the federal application process. It easier than you think to get a federal government job.
- I assumed you want to get a federal job but understand that you have a veteran's preference of 5 percent or 10 percent (this is usually the case).
- I assumed you don't understand which federal jobs you can apply for.
- I assumed you do not know the language of the resume world.
- I assumed you're a fighter.

THE INFORMATION PROVIDED IS *NOT* A SUBSTITUTION FOR LEGAL ADVICE (PLEASE READ THIS CLOSELY)

I am often asked whether I am an attorney. I am not. That question bothers me more than it should. There are so many people like me who help veterans and have learned how to fight against veteran's preference violations. People think you need an attorney from the beginning of a complaint. This is not true. In fact what you do in the beginning stages of your application determines how your case will be handled. If you get nervous easily or can't speak in front of people, I say, with reservations, that you should eventually get an attorney. However, if you can write well enough, you can do motion law arguments and never have to say a word. Most—if not all—of the work in these cases involves writing. You can represent yourself and do a good job if you have the right tools. This book is more than your starting point. There are a lot of attorneys who will take your case and do not have a clue about the federal government's human resource practices. The master of your situation is you—the preference eligible. If you start looking for an attorney, ask around and learn about his or her background. The handbook will put you leaps and bounds ahead of the game if you must fight.

Here is a story of what happened to a friend of mine who hired an attorney. A young female veteran hired an allegedly experienced attorney who said he had handled veteran's preference violation cases. The attorney charged $200 an hour for his consultation (the trick). The fee became part of the attorney's fees if the veteran decided to retain the attorney's services. The attorney let my friend just talk her little preference-eligible head off. The veteran explained her circumstances to the best of her ability (without knowledge of this book), and the high-priced attorney dazzled her with his lawyerly language. The veteran was convinced she found the right attorney. The veteran then walked out of the attorney's office and handed his secretary her credit card. The secretary charged $3,800 of the required $4,000 fee to handle her veteran's preference violation. (Remember the trick—a lure—of $200 for the consultation fee.) People don't have money to blow, and some attorneys are banking on just that—that you don't have the money to keep having consultations until you find the right fit. Eventually, the attorney filed the proper paperwork with the Merit System Protection Board, dazzling the veteran just a bit more. Well, that's where it all pretty much ended. The veteran could not afford interrogatories, requests for production of documents, depositions, admit and deny requests, and more, so no discovery took place to determine whether a preference-right violation had occurred. All the attorney's fees were tied up in the procedural stage. Believe it or not, thousands of veteran's preference cases are filed yearly, but they get dismissed or overlooked for similar reasons. There are plenty of experts who are not attorneys. If you don't believe me, take a look at the agents of nonprofit veterans' organizations who work on the behalf of veterans. They help file disability claims, petition Congress, start organizations dedicated to veterans—the list is endless. I have spent many years wondering why so many veterans who want to work do not have the federal jobs they seek. I served in the Marine Corps, and no one told me about job opportunities with the federal government until I was sitting in a room during a transition assistant program (TAP). TAP is a great program, and I really do not know of any other field where such a program is offered. However, it just didn't have the follow through that was needed to get a good grip on understanding the job market, especially the federal sector. While I was sitting in that room with many other veterans, I briefly wondered where they were headed. Did they know their future? Many were oblivious, and from what I hear, many military personnel transitioning back into the civilian world are still clueless about the opportunities that exist in the federal government. Uncle Sam still needs you, your spouse, and your mother so why not learn of the many opportunities of federal sector jobs. Upon going through the process of getting out, I distinctly remember walking into a career counselor's office in Twenty-Nine Palms, California, and asking about www.usajobs.gov. The counselor was not very helpful, despite the fact he had used that very site to get his federal sector job. This website is the gateway to your opportunities with a federal agency. The jobs you see listed are not hoaxes. They are real positions that must be filled. That counselor really didn't tell me much other than how to log on and start looking for positions I qualified for. My goal is to show you how your preference-eligible rights apply to your opportunities with the federal government. Don't get the idea that because you served your country honorably that a federal agency will hand you a job. There are hundreds of thousands of nonveterans against whom you are competing, and they are not playing. Civilians know some of the best resume tricks ever invented, but they too struggle without the right information. Nonetheless, civilians have the same problem as veterans when it comes to understanding federal sector resumes. I'll demonstrate what many civilians don't know about federal resumes. Civilians bring a credential you likely don't have: a college degree. Most veterans' military experience usually exceeds the experience of a civilians' work experience, and your military experience regardless of job titles must be considered if you place it in your resume. Consider your training and leadership experience from the time you stepped on those yellow footprints and the many billets you held during your service. If you were put in charge to mop floors then you have management experience. Think critically. Get creative! Think closely—you actually work for the federal government, so you have an upper hand. I'll show you where to go to fit your military experience into a federal job resume. Talk to civilian employees on military bases and you will find they can help you plan ahead. The best part is that knowing how to assert your veteran's preference rights will put you over the top.

MY NONLEGAL HUMBLE ADVICE

It's all about timing.

As soon as you receive notice you were not selected, determine whether you have a viable veteran's preference right violation. If you do not know if a violation has occurred you should file a complaint anyway and get some good learning experience out of the process. You may surprise yourself! (Refer to the case law excerpts I list below.)

As soon as you believe your preference rights have been violated, contact the agency and ask who was selected. If you can, send an email.

Be polite but assertive, and conduct your investigation as though you were a police detective. When you make contact the following will suffice: "I recently applied for (input job announcement and vacancy number), and I would like to know where I appeared on the certificate of eligible." Keep all records. Determine if the person selected was a veteran. If so, ask what the person's disability rating was, if it applies, and then ask why you were not selected. Do this over a series of emails. Remember it's easier to catch flies with honey. You may also find you were more qualified than the person who was selected. If so, you should file a complaint with the equal employment officer with the agency.

If the point of contact you are dealing with begins to get irritated ask the agency representative what the procedure is to make a request for records under the Freedom of Information Act. (See example in the appendix.) Make plenty of pertinent Request for Information requests. Do not request what you do not need, and be specific in your request.

Contact the US Department of Labor, and file a complaint for veteran's preference rights violations. If the agency representative starts avoiding you then you have plenty of reason to begin your complaint with the US Department of Labor.

After the Department of Labor has completed its investigation, file your complaint with the Merit System Protection Board in a timely fashion. (If there are any issues with what you filed, you or an attorney can amend the complaint later. Just get the complaint filed.)

Contact an attorney who does not charge for consultations and ask whether you should bring additional charges under Title VII for violations of the 1964 Civil Rights Act. (By this time, you should have the information you requested related to the Request for Information, which will save you money if you have to hire an attorney.)

If you can find a representative who is not an attorney who has experienced veteran's preference violations and actually went through the appeal process, use them instead of an attorney to help you through the discovery process. These people know the game. You may get lucky and find an attorney who has performed as a representative and who is also a veteran. Let the attorney file for a substitution. Please note that you can find attorneys who specialize in MSPB and EEO litigation.

What Type of Education Do I Need

There are two scenarios veterans should consider: the type of education needed and location, location, location.

The type of education you need should be based on the field of your choice, but veterans should not limit the amount of coursework in specialty areas. Complete the coursework first that relates to the specialty work for the position(s) you are seeking. Many positions in the federal government substitute education for experience. Specialty areas are fields such as accounting, teaching, law, and nursing, etc. Many veterans I speak with want to go into law enforcement. In my opinion, a degree in law enforcement is great, but if you're going to work in law enforcement, you will be gaining the experience you'll need as a law enforcement officer without obtaining a degree in the field of law enforcement. Truthfully, federal, state, and local law enforcement agencies, for the most part, do not have a particular educational requirement. They just want you to have a bachelor's degree in any field even if they don't require a degree. It would behoove veterans in this type of situation to get a degree in the field of business administration or public administration with a focus in finance or accounting. Many federal government jobs will require a minimum of twenty-four credit hours in a specialty area as a substitute for a complete degree. Otherwise, many federal government positions require a bachelor's degree in any field from an accredited educational institution and at least twenty-four hours in (business-related) courses in any of the following fields: accounting, business, finance, law, contracts, purchasing, economics, industrial management, marketing, quantitative methods, or organization and management. This requirement can be obtained within the degree or in addition to the degree. Review as many job announcements as possible, and get a good feel for the type of education you will need.

A word on location. Many federal job locations in the United States are hotspots, and many applicants are seeking to relocate to these areas. Avoid hotspots if you are seeking a position that is not technical until you are in the system. Your chances will increase dramatically. Hotspots are usually the areas that offer locality pay. Visit www.opm.gov/policy-data-oversight/pay-leave/salaries-wages/2012/general-schedule for a list of these areas. I was talking to a veteran who told me that he applied for the same position numerous times in Phoenix, Atlanta, Brooklyn, and Los Angeles. Finally, the veteran applied for the same position in the middle of nowhere (Yuma, Arizona), and he was hired immediately. I have heard this numerous times.

Excepted Service vs. Competitive Service: Veterans Beware

As a veteran, you should know whether a federal job announcement is excepted or competitive service.

All VRAs are hired under excepted service appointments. Most VEOA appointments are otherwise in the competitive service. After two years of satisfactory service, the agency must convert the VRA appointment to career or career-conditional appointment. Usually, excepted service positions are with agencies such as the CIA, FBI, or Defense Intelligence Agency. Excepted service rules do not apply to veterans if they are not hired under VRA appointments. Typically, excepted service agencies require investigations that take longer than a year to complete. Only about 40 percent of all federal jobs are in the excepted service category. The others are called competitive service. Competitive service appointments are afforded protections under the guidelines of the Office of Personnel Management, while some appointments under excepted service agencies are not. The drawback of excepted service involves limited interchange with competitive service positions. However, many excepted service agencies have an agreement with the Office of Personnel Management, but this is not a universal practice. The disadvantage between the two services is all provisions that apply for competitive service appointment do not apply in the excepted service.

There are two main advantages of VRA appointments. One, veterans are converted to career conditional after two years. Nonveterans are converted after three years. Two, veterans may appeal prohibited personnel actions after one year of service. Nonveterans must wait until they are career/career-conditional.

The main importance of these advantages is that if preference eligible is facing removal, he or she may challenge the appeal to the MSPB. Keep in mind a veteran (regardless of time in service) can immediately appeal to the MSPB if he or she is being removed for performance related issues. Veterans with a disability may be protected from disability discrimination during the probationary period. Let your supervisor know (by email) that you are having performance problems relating to your service connected disability. You may also be protected from termination even if your disability is not service connected.

Major Excepted Services Organizations

Federal Reserve System Board of Governors 20th and C Sts, NW Washington DC 20551	**Federal Aviation Administration** Employment AHR-19A 800 Independence Ave SW Washington DC 20591	**Central Intelligence Agency** Office of Personnel Washington DC 20505
Defense Intelligence Agency Civilian Personnel Office The Pentagon Washington DC 20340-3042	**U.S. Department of State** (Foreign Service positions) PO Box 9317 Rosslyn Station, Arlington VA 22219	**Federal Bureau of Investigation** J. Edgar Hoover Bldg, Rm. 6647 10th St & Pennsylvania Ave NW Washington DC 20571
General Accounting Office 441 G St NW, Room 1157 Washington DC 20548	**International Agency for Development** 2401 E St NW, Room 1127 Washington DC 20523	**National Security Agency** College Relations Branch Fort Meade MD 20750
Nuclear Regulatory Commission Division of Personnel Resources and Employment Program Branch Washington DC 20555	**Postal Rates Commission** Administrative Office, Suite 300 Washington DC 20268-0001	**Tennessee Valley Authority** Knoxville Office Complex 400 West Summit Hill Drive Knoxville TN 37902
U.S. Mission to the United Nations 700 United Nations Plaza New York NY 10001	**Department of Veterans Affairs** (Health Research Services Administration) 810 Vermont Avenue NW Washington DC 20420	**U.S. Supreme Court, Personnel Office** First St NE Washington DC 20543
Administrative Office of the U.S. Courts Personnel Division, Room L701 Washington DC 20544	**U.S. Claims Court** 717 Madison Place NW Washington DC 20005	**U.S. Senate** Senate Placement Office Hart Senate Ofc. Bldg, Rm. 142B Washington DC 20510
U.S. House of Representatives House Placement Office House Office Bldg Annex 2,Room 219 3rd and D Sts SW Washington DC 20515-6609	**Library of Congress** Employment Office Room 107 Madison Building Washington DC 20540	

Reasons to Read the
Delegated Examining Operations Handbook

That federal agencies play too many games is the main reason. I know you're not going to let me get away with just that, so I will explain. There are many nuances (that are simple mistakes on your part) that you should be aware of that may keep you from competing for federal jobs. I like to give real-life stories, and here is a good one. Keep in mind that a lot of these cases don't even make it out of the gate, and you'll never hear or read about them elsewhere. Several years ago, I received a phone call from a young Purple Heart recipient who nearly lost his life serving in the Marine Corps (Marines are called devil dogs). I must mention he is a real hard charger. He told me he applied for a position with a federal agency and that he received email notification that he was found nonqualified for a position. The position required only a minimum of a bachelor's degree in any field or related experience. This devil dog actually held the same position as a police officer for which he was applying under the title of the federal job announcement. The agency notified the Marine he was found nonqualified because he did not submit a required form. I instructed the Marine to contact the agency and ask to be allowed to submit the missing document. The agency ignored his request and filled the position.

Here is the problem: On page seventy-seven of the Delegated Examine Operations Handbook, it states the following:

"GENERAL RULE"

"An application is incomplete if an applicant:

1. Does not submit a required form or other material, as specified in the job announcement;
2. Fails to respond to questions that he or she must answer before any action can be taken; or

3. Submits insufficient information concerning education or experience.

You may rate incomplete applications based on the information provided, or you may ask the applicant to furnish the missing information. Whichever option you choose, however, *you should apply it consistently for all applicants* for any specific position or competitor inventory."

These are clear instruction delegated to federal agencies by the US Office of Personnel Management. The agency should have accepted the documents if not at least out of courtesy for this Purple Heart recipient. He filed a complaint with the US Department of Labor and lost. However, he won his case on the day his complaint was filed with the MSPB. The board told the agency to visit page seventy-seven of the DEOH. Like I said, this case did not even make it out of the gate. This is one of the many reasons preference eligibles should read the DEOH.

Google OF-306. Always submit this form with your federal applications. OF-306 is a form that helps an agency determine your suitability for federal employment. It is not always optional, so just get into the habit of submitting it each time you apply for a federal job.

Another reason to read the DEOH is that many code words exist in the DEOH. The sooner you understand that your resume has to break the Office of Personnel Management (OPM) code word barrier, the better off you'll be. The federal government has guidelines for everything. Well, almost everything. Actually, that's a good thing if you think about it. It helps minimize discretion and veteran's preference violations.

A Deep-Dark Secret to Getting Your Resume through Human Resources

The secret is that the government has literally laid out what your resume must say. Take a look at the Standards by Occupational Series.

The Power of OPM's Rule of Three

It is important to get your education, experience, and job-related experience into your resume so that your name reaches the top of every certificate of eligible. Keep a journal, and document of everything you do while on active duty. This includes duties such as fire watch, cleaning floors, squad leader, platoon guide, and more. Everything veterans do in the military involves managing a program. Many agencies hire management and program analysts. If veterans can get their name in the top three of a certificate of eligible, it is next to impossible not to get hired, especially if you apply for jobs vacancies that have many openings under the same announcement. The power of the rule of three makes it next to impossible for a selection official to overlook your name on a job announcement seeking multiple hires.

CUTTING DOWN ON THE CONFUSION

Most people are confused by how applicants are ranked on a certificate of eligible. Veterans have an added benefit beyond the five or ten points added to a test. Let's say that as a preference eligible, you applied for a position with a federal agency and that there are three certificates issued under one certificate. One certificate means a VRA, VEOA, or Merit Promotion. Now, under a VEOA certificate, there is a qualified list, a best qualified list, and a well-qualified list. Well-qualified is the highest. Let's say the cut-off score for the qualified list is eighty to eighty-seven, the cut-off score for best qualified is eighty-eight to ninety-five, and the cut-off score for well qualified is ninety-six to one hundred. In most cases, if not all, the agency decides to use the well-qualified list, and your score as a veteran in the well-qualified category is only ninety-six compared to a nonveteran who may have scored one hundred. Even though your score as a veteran is lower than the nonveteran, as a veteran, you are placed the highest in that category, and you must be selected if another preference eligible is not selected. One of two things may occur. One, if the agency decides to select the nonveteran over a 30 percent or more veteran, it must first make a passover request to the Office of Personnel Management. Or two, if the veteran was in the top three, the rule of three applies, and you should file with the Department of Labor and then the MSPB if you believe the person selected was either not a veteran or had lower preference points. Different decisions are made by MSPB on whether a veteran must be selected if they fall within the top three of a certificate, so file. Again, follow up with the human resources department or the selecting official. If he or she is helpful and provides you with the information you need to review the decision that was made, and you determine something is not right, file a complaint. The laws that protect your rights lean on the issue of whether you believe your rights were violated. Preference-eligible applicants cannot make that determination if the agency does not disclose the information you need to make that decision so file.

How Pay Increases Work

I get this question a lot. Most well-qualified applicants who would usually apply don't because they don't understand the progressive pay scale of the federal government. The pay does not seem to be a lot for many general schedule positions, but pay attention to the promotion potential. Let's say you are interested in a position as criminal investigator, and you notice the job announcement says GS-7 to GS-9. That simply means the federal agency will hire you either as a GS-7 or GS-9. Now, the promotional potential should be your focus because the promotion potential for a criminal investigator is usually GS-12 or GS-13. Research the occupational series of your choice and determine what the promotional potential is for your career field. Keep in mind, though, that you may find that some agencies have different grade levels of promotion potential. For instance, the Air Force lists job announcements for contract specialist with a promotional potential of GS-15 for many of its duty stations. However, the Department of Veterans Affairs may list the contract specialist position with a promotion potential of only GS-9. This may be for many reasons, but do not worry about that for now. If you decide to take a GS-9 position, you can always promote to another agency or within the agency to a GS-11 grade as long as you have fifty-two weeks of service prior to the closing date of another job announcement. Therefore, it is possible to promote to GS-15 if you're prepared to jump from agency to agency.

LEARN HOW TO ISLAND HOP TO GET TO THE TOP

My drill instructors would discipline recruits by taking us to different sand pits. They called this island hoping. Let's say that you do get hired by a federal agency, but that it is just not the job you really wanted. For instance, say you get hired by the Department of Veterans Affairs as a GS-5 materials handler, but you want to find a position as a GS-9 contract specialist. Use the experience you have a materials handler and go as far as to do related work of a contract specialist while in the materials handler position. It's not that hard. Once you've been in the materials handler position for fifty-two weeks, rewrite your resume so that it now includes the specialized experience you need for the contract specialist position. You may also get a certificate as a contract specialist. Now that reaches a little further. Remember that those days you served in the military also include specialized experience you need for your resume. As an illustration, let's say that you served as an electrician and that you are now interested in becoming a criminal investigator. It is likely that while serving as an electrician, you did at least one investigation into equipment failure. I found that equipment failure sometimes involved elements such as neglect, which would require you to perform similar functions as a criminal investigator. That's called specialized experience. Once you get creative, you will realize you have the specialized experience to get hired by the federal government.

Where to Find the Code Words for Federal Resume Writing

Put on your thinking cap. This is where you get very creative. I cannot express the importance of this part enough, so please pay attention. Go to www.usajobs.gov. Click the blue Search button. On the next page, scroll down to the section that says Occupational Series. Now take some time to research this section. Keep in mind that the job you may be seeking at this time may not be available when you conduct your actual job search. Be careful about the grade level you accept upon hire. After you have finished your research, chose an occupational series and search for it on Google. The secret that goes beyond the understanding of just inputting code words to get past the resume phase is to find OPM's language within your occupational series. OPM tells every federal agency the who, what, when, where, and how. For example, Google [Human Resource Management 0201 + OPM]. "Human Resource Management 0201" is found within the occupational series. Always use "+ OPM" to help you find the occupational series of your choice. You will notice many different selections, but look for a PDF. Here is an example of the website to help you better understand what these occupational series documents may look like: https://www.opm.gov/policy-data-oversight/classification-qualifications/classifying-general-schedule-positions/standards/0200/gs0200a.pdf

These documents have every code word you need, and most importantly, they will give you a clear understanding of the occupational series of your interest to help you build a solid resume. For now, just stick with this document and read it closely to get a feel for what you'll be looking for on Google. Then branch out to other occupational series PDFs of your chosen field, and read the documents to get a good feel of the language you need to build your own resume. Locate and use the language code words from the highest grade level within the occupational series of your field. Pay close attention to the factors and levels, and use this information wisely. Do not cut and paste from these documents—use your brain. Below is a chart of more examples to help you better understand what you will be looking for.

Examples of searches for OPM Standards of Occupational Series. Remember do not cut and Paste from these documents. Use them as a guide line to build the "code word" and language of your own personal resumes. The power of this information will boost your resume tremendously.
Occupational Series: Accounting **Google Search Term: 0510 Accounting + OPM** **Web address: http://nawbc.com/gs%20510%20series.pdf**
Occupational Series: Criminal Investigations **Google Search Term: 1811 Criminal Investigator + OPM** **Web address: http://www.opm.gov/policy-data-oversight/** **classification-qualifications/classifying-general-schedule-positions/** **standards/1800/1800a.pdf**
Occupational Series: Air Craft Operation **Google Search Term: 2181 Air Craft Operation + OPM** **Web address: http://www.opm.gov/policy-data-oversight/** **classification-qualifications/classifying-general-schedule-positions/** **standards/2100/gs2181.pdf**
Occupational Series: Auditing **Google Search Term: 0511 Auditing + OPM** **Web address: https://www.opm.gov/policy-data-oversight/** **classification-qualifications/classifying-general-schedule-positions/** **standards/0500/gs0500pa.pdf**
Occupational Series: Automotive Mechanic **Google Search Term: 5823 Automotive Mechanic + OPM** **Web address: http://www.opm.gov/policy-data-oversight/** **classification-qualifications/classifying-federal-wage-system-** **positions/standards/5800/fws5823.pdf**

Occupational Series: Barbering Google Search Term: 7603 Barbering + OPM Web address: https://www.opm.gov/policy-data-oversight/ classification-qualifications/classifying-federal-wage-system- positions/standards/7600/fws7603.pdf
Occupational Series: All Biological Scientist Google Search Term: 0400 All Biological Scientist + OPM Web address: http://www.opm.gov/policy-data-oversight/ classification-qualifications/classifying-general-schedule-positions/ standards/0400/gs0400p.pdf
Occupational Series: Budget Analysis Google Search Term: 0560 Budget Analysis + OPM Web address: https://www.opm.gov/policy-data-oversight/ classification-qualifications/classifying-general-schedule-positions/ standards/0500/gs0500pa.pdf
Occupational Series: Chaplin Google Search Term: 0060 Chaplin + OPM Web address: http://www.opm.gov/policy-data-oversight/classification- qualifications/classifying-general-schedule-positions/standards/0000/ gs0060.pdf
Occupational Series: Google Search Term: Web address:

DELEGATED EXAMINING OPERATIONS HANDBOOK

This is an OPM manual. It is your best friend and worst enemy if you fail to adopt it as a part of your career. Read and understand it, and you will be much more successful. This is a guide for federal agency examining offices, which is nothing more than the human resources department of a federal agency. You can find it at http://www.opm.gov/policy-data-oversight/

hiring-authorities/competitive-hiring/deo_handbook.pdf or simply Google "delegated examining operations handbook".

How to Use **WWW.USAJOBS.GOV**

This site is the only way you can get hired into nearly any federal agency that exists. I am repeating this because I advised many potential applicants to visit this website, but many do not seem to take me seriously. After finally interviewing many of these people, they tell me they think the website is like any other website because they have used many other sites and have not received any feedback. That is not the case with www.usajobs. gov. Once you apply, you will receive a series of emails notifying you of your status. Likewise, you may check the status of your own applications. This really requires a PowerPoint presentation. Many applicants fail at the use of this site. It looks simple, but there are several things you must know before and after applying. After you have applied, keep a copy of the application you submit because the application manager does not maintain the actual copy you submit. Well, it does, but you will not see the original copy of the application after you submit it. It is important that you maintain a copy for your records because you will find that as you start submitting applications, documents will "accidently" come up missing if you ever complain about your veteran's preference rights being violated. For preference eligibles, be sure to select the button that permits you to select federal employee. If you conduct your search and limit it to only US citizens, you will miss thousands of jobs you are eligible for.

Keep Good Records of All Applications

Keep a folder of all of your job applications. For all your federal applications, be sure to keep a copy of all the forms and questionnaires. Forms include your DD-214, SF-15, OF-306, 30 percent or more letter, cover letter, and transcripts. Always submit a cover letter and include in the letter that you are requesting consideration under the Veterans Recruitment Act. This type of cover letter will serve as evidence if a selecting official later says he or she was not aware of your preference eligibility. Once you have submitted your application, save a copy of the application you submitted. After you have submitted your application and the human resources department puts together the certificate of eligible, it may have overlooked your five-point, ten-point, or 30 percent or more proof for veteran's preference. This includes saving a copy of the locations you choose if the job announcement has multiple locations.

MISSED WORK BECAUSE OF QUALIFIED MILITARY SERVICE

Under the Uniformed Services Employment and Reemployment Rights Act of 1994 (USERRA), if you miss work because of qualified military service, you may be entitled to make up contributions you missed during your military service. If you serve in any of the military reserves talk to your employer about the contributions you may have missed because of your deployments. You only have a certain amount of time to make these contributions so contact your human resource department as soon as possible.

COMMON TYPES OF VETERAN'S PREFERENCE VIOLATIONS

"I am concerned for the security of our great Nation; not so much because of any treat from without, but because of the insidious forces working from within."

—Douglas MacArthur

PASSOVER OF COMPENSABLE-DISABLED PREFERENCE ELIGIBLE VIOLATIONS

In March 2009, the Court of Appeals for the Federal Circuit in *Gingery v. Department of Defense* issued a decision that resulted in requiring federal agencies to apply competitive service rules to passover preference eligibles with a 30 percent or more compensable service-connected disability for excepted service positions subject to the appointment procedures in 5 C.F.R. part 302. Selecting officials must justify their decision to passover a preference eligible in order to select a nonpreference eligible in every position you apply for if you are a 30 percent or more preference eligible veteran. Spouses and mothers of certain disabled veterans may qualify under this new law if they are not selected over a nonpreference eligible applicant. Selecting officials may not request a passover because a nonveteran is better qualified than a preference eligible. The reason for a passover must relate directly to the veteran's qualifications and/or fitness for employment. Many selecting officials take the chance that veterans will not inquire about where they were ranked on a certificate of eligible list. Passover-request violations frequently occur. Many human resources components of the federal government now require selecting officials to submit a passover request to their regional human resource divisions before they submit the passover request to the Office of Personnel Management. For a copy of the memo implementing this requirement, go to http://www.chcoc.gov/Transmittals/TransmittalDetails.aspx?TransmittalId=2119

Rule of Three Violations

Selecting officials must hire a preference eligible from the highest three eligibles listed on a certificate of eligible. The highest three must be available for the job. If the original highest three are not available, the agency must either reconstruct the certificate or select the next highest available candidate. The agency may not passover a preference-eligible candidate to select a lower raking nonpreference eligible or nonpreference eligible with the same or lower score.

The Office of Personnel Management provided the following examples at http://www.opm.gov/policy-data-oversight/veterans-services/vet-guide.

Example: if the top person on a certificate is a ten-point disabled veteran (CP or CPS) and the second and third persons are five-point preference eligibles, the appointing authority may choose any of the three. (It is unclear whether a passover request must be made if another veteran is selected with less than 30 percent eligibility over a 30 percent or more veteran. However, a spouse or mother of a qualified disabled veteran may not be selected over a preference-eligible veteran.)

Example: If the top person on a certificate is a ten-point disabled veteran (CP or CPS), the second person is not a preference eligible, and the third person is a five-point preference eligible, the appointing authority may choose either of the preference eligibles. The appointing authority may not pass over the ten-point disabled veteran to select the nonpreference eligible unless an objection has been sustained.

Veterans Recruitment Act Violations

In my many years of experience, I have that VRA violations occur frequently. Veteran's preference itself has been referred to as a bona fide qualification. In other words, selecting officials are not required to use VRA certificates. However, it is arguable if a veteran can prove that selecting officials are purposefully overlooking the use of the VRA. I have personally discovered on several occasions selecting officials setting aside a VRA certificate and using VEOA certificates to avoid more qualified applicants. Selecting officials are not required to use VRA certificates.

Here are several reasons selecting officials do not use VRA certificate:

- Selecting official selects a person who was referred by an existing employee. This is typically called word of mouth hiring.
- A veteran is severely disabled.
- A veteran has more education than other applicants.

Several years ago, I handled a complaint in which a veteran had a master's degree and ten years of experience. The veteran submitted her proof of 30 percent or more eligibility. The agency responded to a Department of Labor complaint and responded by saying that the veteran did not submit her proof of eligibility. However, the Department of Labor found in favor of the veteran. The veterans (several) selected were less than 30 percent disabled, had less than seven months of experience in the field, and held associate's degrees. We later discovered that all the veterans selected were referrals.

Outside of Location Violations

Eligibles who are eligible for preference may apply to a job announcement that limits candidates outside of the local commuting area. For example, if a federal agency posts a job announcement for applicants in only the local commuting area of San Francisco, California, and you currently live in Petersburg, Virginia, as a preference eligible, you can apply. Many human resources specialist do not know this rule and will disqualify these applications without knowing the rules that apply to veterans' preference. If this occurs, simply call the agency and request for your application to be reconsidered and explain to the human resources specialist your eligibility status. If at all possible, respond to the Notice of Results email and request reconsideration.

Merit Promotion Vacancy Announcement Violations

Veterans with veterans' preference may apply for merit promotion job announcements. A merit promotion announcement is an announcement open to only internal applicants. The law allows preference eligibles to compete with internal applicants. Under this particular law, selecting officials may select any candidate. (It is not clear if the Rule of Three applies to merit promotion announcements.) If the veteran is selected, the VEOA eligible is given a career or career-conditional appointment.

Suitability/Fitness for Duty Violations

A veteran who is eligible for veteran's preference can be eliminated from consideration only if the agency's human resources department where the veteran applied has been permitted to do so by the OPM. Agencies have been delegated authority by OPM for determining suitability determinations in accordance with 5 CFR Part 731. However, OPM is prohibited by law from delegating passover procedures to an agency when the veteran is 30 percent or more disabled. For more information, see 5 U.S.C. 3312, 3318. The agency must follow OPM's procedures to passover a veteran who is not 30 percent or more disabled. What typically happens in a suitability/fitness for duty violations is an agency has made a determination that the veteran is not able to perform certain duties based on the veteran's service-connected disability. Veterans have the right to object to the agency determinations. The agency must notify the veteran in writing when the agency makes an objection to hiring or retaining a veteran. The veteran must object within fifteen days of the notice.

Criminal History Discrimination

Many veterans end up getting involved in crime. I can't count the number of times I have met incarcerated veterans. A few of the veterans were serving time for robbing banks. When I asked why they had committed these crimes, they are foolish enough to say that they used their military experience to pull off the job. Even people with criminal records are hired by the federal government for jobs that do not interfere with certain types of security clearances. Keep in mind that even a veteran with a criminal record will likely not be hired to carry a firearm so your federal applications should be geared toward jobs that do not require such criteria. Laws governing criminal history discrimination are under the jurisdiction of Equal Employment Opportunity Offices. The Merit System Protection Board reviews criminal history discrimination under the purview of suitability claims.

Where to Go When Your Veteran's Preference Rights are Violated

"Never tell people how to do things. Tell them what to do,
and they will surprise you with their ingenuity."

—George S. Patton

Online Submission of Violations

To submit a veteran's preference claim, go to https://vets1010.dol.gov.

Veteran's Preference Violation Complaints to the MSPB

Do not confuse what an appeal is to the MSPB. As a preference-eligible veteran, spouse, or parent, you are vested in filing an appeal to the MSPB for an alleged preference violation. Many veterans confuse what an appeal is because they believe that filing an appeal with the board means objecting to a standing decision. Essentially, what you're doing is appealing a decision by a federal agency. It's not a bad thing. Basically what you are doing is appealing a decision by a federal agency that you believe is not correct. Your veteran's preference rights gave you the ability to file an appeal on a decision not to hire you even though you are not an employee of a federal agency. It could be as simple as the federal agency did not receive your DD214, SF-15, veteran's preference letter of 30 percent or more, or other documentation that may prove your status as a qualified veteran.

Appeals under the Uniformed Services Employment and Reemployment Rights Act of 1994 Have No Time Limit for Filing (5 C.F.R. § 1208.12)

Your rights to reemployment include reemployment in the private sector. The private sector is an employer other than the federal, state, or local government. Therefore, if you have joined the armed forces and you were employed in your community before you left home, you are entitled to seek reemployment with that employer. Many recruits make the mistake of resigning or quitting their jobs before joining the armed forces and miss out on the opportunity for reemployment.

Mixed Motive Cases and Veteran's Preference Violations

"It is fatal to enter a war without the will to win it"

—Douglas MacArthur

Mixed Motive Cases

For purposes of veteran's preference, a mixed motive case is a veteran's preference violation and Title VII claim filed together with the MSPB. Veterans may file a Title VII claim along with a complaint of veteran's preference violation, but there is a risk of untimeliness. The better approach is to file a claim with the agencies Equal Employment Opportunity office in the event you believe you have been discriminated on the basis of age, race, national origin, disability, or gender. Veterans typically experience subtle forms of disability discrimination where the persons conducting the interviews ask veterans what their disabilities are. If this occurs, contact the agency's EEO office. The Equal Employment Opportunity Commission (EEOC) has jurisdiction over Title VII claims, but there is no specific law for veteran's disability discrimination. If veterans believe they have been discriminated against on the basis of their disability, the EEO violation is mostly likely under the laws of either the Americans with Disabilities Act or the Rehabilitation Act. I would advise that you speak to an EEO attorney. For judicial economy, the MSPB may hear claims of Title VII if it first establishes that you have filed a nonfrivolous appeal regarding your preference rights. When you file a claim with the MSPB, its first jurisdiction is to establish your veterans preference rights appeal, not your Title VII rights.

As an illustration (and these are considered facts of a case), several years ago, I was contacted by Tom, a sixty-two-year-old Caucasian male who had retired from a large metropolitan police department. He holds a master's degree in criminal justice/law enforcement administration. He has mountains of civil, administrative, and criminal investigative experience. Most importantly, though, he is a veteran with a 70 percent service-connected disability rating. Tom was not selected several times for a GS-9 1801 series position he applied to with a federal agency. The age limitation of thirty-seven did not apply to the job announcement. The promotion potential for the position was GS-12. Tom filed a VEOA claim with the Department of Labor, which found that the federal agency failed to make a proper passover request to the Office of Personnel Management. The Department of Labor ordered the agency to fix the problem. The agency refused. Tom then received a notice of a right to file with the MSPB, and he did so in a timely fashion. Tom filed his veteran's preference claim and an age discrimination claim with the MSPB because the agency hired a person who was younger than forty and less qualified.

How to File a Federal Sector EEO Charge

Discrimination against veterans arises more than you know, especially discrimination on the basis of a service-connected disability. A complaint of discrimination against a federal agency is not filed with the EEOC. The EEOC handles private sector complaints of discrimination. A private sector employer is defined as an employer other than a federal agency. When you file an EEO complaint against a federal agency, you must file within forty-five days of the date the incident occurred. If it was a personnel action, you must file within forty-five days of the date you became aware of the discriminatory action or from the date of the personnel action. The forty-five-day time limitation usually starts when you have been given notice of nonselection. This applies to federal employees and applicants for federal employment. Our advice is to contact the EEO counselor at the agency where you applied on the date you become aware of the situation. Simply call the agency and ask for the EEO counselor. Keep in mind how federal agencies play with the statutory time frame of forty-five days. This may be done by sending you an email notifying you of the results of your nonselection. This is typically your start date of harm.

Here are several suggestions:

- Always contact the Equal Employment Officer (EEO) counselor by certified mail (or by email if you're a federal employee or applicant for federal employment). If you must send an email, do so to the email address listed on the job announcement.
- Fill out the appropriate forms and submit them to the EEO counselor. Be sure to keep an accurate record of the date you made contact with the counselor.
- The EEO counselor will notify the federal agency that you have filed a charge and informally attempt to resolve your complaint.
- If the complaint is not informally resolved within thirty days, you may formally file. If the complaint is not informally resolved, the thirty-day time frame may be extended at your request or that of the counselor, under limited circumstances. Our advice is to not agree to an extension and formally file at a later date if the complaint cannot be resolved.
- **5)** Once you receive the EEO counselor's Notice of Final Interview, you must file your formal complaint within fifteen calendar days of your receipt of the notice.
- **6)** After you have filed your formal complaint, the agency will contract with an EEO investigator. This is your time to tell your story. You should call around and talk to an attorney who has experience in federal sector discrimination complaints. Many attorneys do not understand the internal policy and procedures of federal agencies, so you don't want to run into an attorney and pay for his learning experience.

- 7) The EEO investigator is persistent. Here's why: In the federal sector, you will be given an opportunity to request a final agency decision (FAD), or you may request a hearing before an EEOC administrative judge. If your complaint is on the basis of sexual orientation, gender identity, or parental status, your report of investigation file will be reviewed by the agency's final investigative decision board. Do not request a FAD. Many people fail at this stage, and if you decide to file an appeal in a federal district court, you are going to be fighting an uphill battle. The first thing you should do is to request a hearing before an EEOC judge, but do not let the judge make a decision on your case. Get your case out of the administrative judge's hand and away from a final agency decision, and file in the federal district court within your jurisdiction.

Needed Legislation

To repair the damage that has been done and to bring back the spirit of President Eisenhower's intent, federal agencies need to be accountable for the following:

- Require federal agencies to combine all certifications when one or more certificate of eligible exists and permit veterans unlimited competition between grades by eliminating the fifty-two-week limitation.
- Require agencies to notify preference-eligible applicants of where they were ranked on each on each certificate of eligible.

CASE LAW EXAMPLES

This section gives you pertinent excerpts of case law decisions made by the MSPB. I will summarize how the board applied its decision and how it relates to your veteran's preference rights. Each quote below is taken directly from a decision I found in a veteran's preference case.

Ask yourself how you could use each example for your particular situation.

CASE LAW EXAMPLE 1

How initial appeals are determined by the board.

"An initial decision must identify all material issues of fact and law, summarize the evidence, resolve issues of credibility, and include the administrative judge's conclusions of law and his legal reasoning, as well as the authorities on which that reasoning rests." *Spithaler v. Office of Personnel Management*, 1 M.S.P.R. 587, 589 (1980).

This is very powerful case. Get very creative with it. After you have filed your case with the MSPB, let's say that you allege that a federal agency violated your veteran's preference. During discovery, you established that the agency did in fact have a copy of your disability letter (30 percent or more), which certified your right to veteran's preference in federal applications. However, the human resources specialist who reviewed your application submitted an affidavit to the MSPB that certifies the agency did not receive your 30 percent or more letter. This is a disputed fact. Nonetheless, you provided overwhelming evidence: a copy of the job application you submitted, a copy of your fax transmission, your own affidavit, and an affidavit of a witness who certifies he or she was with you when you submitted the 30 percent or more letter. Many times, the MSPB will ignore your overwhelming evidence and make a decision against you without ruling on the credibility of your evidence. The MSPB seems to put more weight on the evidence of the agency. Don't let this happen. The MSPB is required to summarize, with legal reasoning, each piece of material evidence you submit. Make the MSPB do its job. If you submit an affidavit as evidence in support of your claim, the MSPB is required to analyze and provide you with legal reasoning for accepting or rejecting your evidence.

Case law example 2

Element iii discussed below is the most difficult to prove.

The board has held that in order to establish jurisdiction over a VEOA appeal, an appellant must: (1) show that she exhausted her remedy with DOL; and (2) make nonfrivolous allegations that (i) she is a preference eligible within the meaning of VEOA; (ii) the action at issue took place on or after the October 30, 1998, enactment date of VEOA; and (iii) the agency violated her rights under a statute or regulation relating to veterans' preference. (This is called a prima facia, and you must meet all of its elements before your case can move forward.)

For the most part, this prima facia is self-explanatory. However, under element iii, it is best to determine which area of law you believe was violated. My suggestion is that you get on the phone and get as many free legal consultations you can or call the Department of Labor and get help to determine which regulation was violated.

Case law example 3

The Department of Labor has sixty days to resolve your appeal.

"VEOA's requirement that she exhaust her remedy with the Department of Labor, she must establish that: (1) she filed a complaint with the

Secretary of Labor; and (2) the Secretary of Labor was unable to resolve the complaint within 60 days or has issued a written notification that the Secretary's efforts have not resulted in resolution of the complaint." *Garcia v. Department of Agriculture*, 110 M.S.P.R. 371, ¶ 9 (2009).

This came about because this veteran either filed her VEOA complaint with the MSPB too soon (before sixty days) or the veteran failed to first file her veteran's preference violation with the Department of Labor. You must file your complaint with the Department of Labor and then the MSPB. Now, if you have other issues, such as age, disability, race, or national origin, then you should preserve those Title VII rights by filing a complaint with the agency's Equal Employment Opportunity office.

Case Law example 4

The agency has to select among the most qualified.

"Specifically, the appellant asserted that the agency violated the 'tie-breaking' rules, apparently by name requesting either or both Gonzalo Rios, a ten-point veteran, and Linda Anderson, a five-point veteran with the same ranking as the appellant, although their names did not appear on the first hiring certificate, which resulted in her not being selected for either of the two positions." *Slater v. US Postal Service*, 112 M.S.P.R. 28, ¶ 6 (2009) (stating that the board uses a liberal pleading standard for allegations of veterans' preference violations in a VEOA appeal); see also *Gingery*, 110 M.S.P.R. 83, ¶ 15; cf. *Morales v. Department of Homeland Security*, No. 2012-3004, 2012 WL 1385963, at *2 (Fed. Cir. Apr. 9, 2012) (finding no entitlement to relief on the merits of the appellant's VEOA appeal because "[t]here is no restriction on the agency's ability to choose one preference-eligible candidate over another, so long as the candidate selected is among the 'highest three eligibles on the [hiring] certificate.'")

This case law is self-explanatory.

Case law example 5

Don't be late. The MSPB grants extensions only in extenuating circumstances. "The 15-day filing deadline set forth in 5 U.S.C. § 3330a(d)(1)(B) for filing a VEOA appeal with the Board is subject to equitable tolling, and an employee's failure to file a Board VEOA appeal within 15 days after receiving written notification from the Secretary of Labor of the results of the Secretary's investigation of the appellant's VEOA complaint does not summarily foreclose the Board from exercising jurisdiction to review the appeal." *Gingery*, 110 M.S.P.R. 83, ¶ 24; see *Kirkendall*, 479 F.3d at 835-44; *Willingham v. Department of the Navy*, 118 M.S.P.R. 21, ¶ 15 n.4 (2012).

This case law is self-explanatory.

Case law example 6

Keep track of all your records because agencies do play games.

The Court explained in *Irwin*, 498 U.S. at 96, that Federal courts have "typically extended equitable relief only sparingly" and that the Court had allowed equitable tolling in situations where the complainant "has actively pursued his judicial remedies by filing a defective pleading during the statutory period" or where the complainant has been "induced or tricked by his adversary's misconduct into allowing the filing deadline to pass. Because the administrative judge did not consider whether equitable tolling is applicable to complaint 002, we are remanding for such consideration." *Gingery*, 110 M.S.P.R. 83, ¶ 24.

This case law is self-explanatory.

Case law example 7

Ensure you provide proof of your preference rating.

"If a veteran is receiving compensation for a disability of 10 percent or more, as the appellant claims that he is, his name ranks above those of others referred for consideration." 5 U.S.C. § 3313(2); *Brandt v. Department of the Air Force*, 103 M.S.P.R. 671, ¶ 6 (2006); 5 C.F.R. § 332.401(b).

If you discover that another applicant was selected who was in the same category and did not have a preference rating of 10 percent or more, your rights have been violated.

Case law example 8

Be careful of special appointments, including the VRA.

Special types of appointments are made with the intent of converting the employee to an appointment in the competitive service and provide noncompetitive conversion eligibility if the employee has satisfied eligibility requirements. Those requirements include a demonstration of satisfactory performance or training, and constitute the 'probationary or trial period' referred to in 5 U.S.C. 7511(a)(1)(C)(i). Employees under these appointments have no procedural or appeal rights, but gain such rights upon conversion to the competitive service. These special appointments include those made under the Presidential Management Intern Program, the Student Work-Study Program ('co-ops'), Veterans Readjustment Appointments (VRA), certain Schedule A appointments of the severely disabled, and others.

This is another reason why you need to keep track of your employment records. I handled a case once where a veteran was terminated for breach of security after one year of employment. However, there were no records produced by the agency nor signed by the veteran that proved the veteran was hired under a VRA appointment. Remember VRA appointments require two years of a probationary periods. The agency used to their advantage knowing the veteran was a veteran to be able to justify a termination without legal standing because of the laws under VRA. Don't let this case law scare you away from applying under the VRA because most terminations are illegal unless the employee was grossly negligent. During your probationary period, you are entitled to quarterly assessments, and most agencies don't do them. This is failure to train.

Case law example 8

"In this context, a preference eligible generally means a veteran who served on active duty in the armed forces during a war or in a campaign or expedition for which a campaign badge has been authorized, or during certain other designated periods; a disabled veteran; or, in some cases, a widow or widower, spouse, or mother of a veteran." 5 U.S.C. § 2108(3); see *Alley v. US Postal Service*, 100 M.S.P.R. 283, ¶ 6 (2005).

A spouse may claim veteran's preference if the disabled veteran is 100 percent. However, a spouse of a veteran may not be selected over an actual veteran.

Case law example 9

A veteran on probation in some case may have appeal rights.

An individual who meets the definition of an 'employee' in 5 U.S.C. § 7511(a) (1) may challenge her removal from the federal service by filing an appeal with the Board. See 5 U.S.C. §§ 7512(1), 7513(d).

Review this law for yourself. It varies. I have had preference-eligible veterans win cases for removal during their probationary period.

Case law example 10

The Board affirmed the administrative judge's finding that the appellant did not satisfy the definition of 'employee' set forth in 5 U.S.C.

§ 7511(a)(1)(C)(ii) but remanded on the issue of whether the appellant satisfied the definition of employee set forth in 5 U.S.C. § 7511(a)(1)(C)(i) because there was evidence in the record that she was serving in an initial appointment pending conversion to the competitive service.

Again, this is a situation where the agency denied that the veteran was serving an initial appointment that would entitle the veteran to appeal rights.

Case law example 11

The agency can't use different selection criteria from what it used when it originally rated applicant.

Based on the record before us, we are unable to determine whether the agency removed the original selectee from the position, whether the agency employed the same criteria for selection during the reconstructed selection process that it employed during the original selection process, or whether the agency changed the selection process when it reconstructed the original selection. Indeed, although the agency claims that the appellant's score of 94.69 during the original selection process was only a 'preliminary' score based upon his 'self-assessment,' the record shows that the three top-ranked applicants from the original selection process were forwarded to the selecting official based upon those same, so-called 'preliminary' scores.

This case law is self-explanatory.

Case law example 12

When you win your case, you're entitled to status quo.

The board's authority to remedy noncompliance is broad and far-reaching and functions to ensure that employees or applicants for employment are returned to the status quo ante or the position that they would have been in had the unlawful agency action not occurred. *Phillips v. Department of the Navy*, 114 M.S.P.R. 19, ¶ 7 (2010).

This case law is self-explanatory.

Case law example 13

Under VEOA, you must meet minimum qualifications.

Specifically, the administrative judge found that the record showed that the appellant did not meet the education and experience requirements of the position and that nothing in VEOA mandates that veterans be considered for positions for which they are not qualified.

The more education you have, the better prepared you are to win your case.

Case law example 14

A perfect example of an oversight.

"Given the board's finding that it appeared the appellant would have been the top-ranked applicant had he received a ten-point preference, the board instructed the agency that it would need to go through the pass over procedures—including giving the appellant notice and an opportunity to respond to the Office of Personnel Management (OPM)—before selecting a lower-ranked non-preference-eligible applicant through the reconstructed process." See *Herbert Russell, Appellant, v. Department of Health and Human Services, Agency.*

You cannot image how many certificate of eligible lists I have reviewed and realized the number of veteran's preference violations. If you believe you were qualified, do not be afraid to assert your rights.

Case law example 15

"The court must receive your request for review no later than sixty calendar days after the date of this order. See 5 U.S.C. § 7703(b)(1)(A) (as rev. eff. Dec. 27, 2012). If you choose to file, be very careful to file on time. The court has held that normally it does not have the authority to waive this statutory deadline and that filings that do not comply with the deadline must be dismissed." See *Pinat v. Office of Personnel Management*, 931 F.2d 1544(Fed. Cir. 1991).

If you do not win your case with the board, you have the right to file in the federal district court sixty days after MSPB's decision.

Case law example 16

Some judges are biased and will override your rights, especially pro se litigates.

"An administrative judge's conduct during the course of a board proceeding warrants a new adjudication only if the administrative judge's comments or actions evidence 'a deep-seated favoritism or antagonism that would make fair judgment impossible.'" *Bieber v. Department of the Army*, 287 F.3d 1358, 1362-63 (Fed. Cir. 2002) (quoting *Liteky v. United States*, 510 U.S. 540, 555 [1994]).

If you are able to record the hearing, you should. Most MSPB hearings are held by phone.

Case law example 17

A subsequent discharge may override a new discharge.

"Thus, under board precedent, if an individual is separated from a qualifying period of military service under honorable conditions, a subsequent discharge under other than honorable conditions does not necessarily disqualify him from preference eligible status under 5 U.S.C. § 2108. *Dooley*, 43 M.S.P.R. at 467; see also *Downs v. Department of Veterans Affairs*, 110 M.S.P.R. 139, ¶¶ 5, 10 (2008) (holding that a disabled veteran with an honorable discharge raised nonfrivolous allegations that he was a preference eligible under 5 U.S.C. § 2108(3) despite another discharge under other than honorable conditions)." *William v. Clark* (1991).

Case law example 18

Read the new VOW law signed by President Obama. (This is an example of how laws change.)

"The Board determined that a distinction was to be made between the effect of 'conditional' discharges (discharges that do not complete the individual's obligated service) and unconditional discharges (discharges that occur at a time when the person has completed the service he was obligated to perform). *Id.* at 466-67. Finding that the appellant in Dooley had completed the service he was obligated to perform and found that 'Congress did not expressly define "separated" and found that 'Congress did not expressly define "separated from the armed forces under honorable conditions" as being limited to the ultimate or last period of military service,' and therefore the appellant's qualifying military service followed by unconditional honorable discharges qualified him as a preference eligible under 5 U.S.C. § 2108. Id."

This case law is self-explanatory.

Case law example 19

Stand your ground.

"An allegation of bias by an administrative judge must be raised as soon as practicable after a party has reasonable cause to believe that grounds for disqualification exist and must be supported by an affidavit." *Lee v. US Postal Service*, 48 M.S.P.R. 274, 280-828.

You get the picture.

Case law example 20

You should be overzealous with your written complaint to the Department of Labor.

"To establish exhaustion, the appellant (the veteran) must show that he provided DOL with a summary of the allegations forming the basis of his complaint so that DOL can conduct an investigation." See *Gingery v. Office of 7*, ¶ 14 (2012); *Burroughs v. Department of the Army*, ¶ 9, aff'd, 445 F. App'x 347 (Fed. Cir. 2011).

Do lose out because you didn't say enough in your complaint.

Case law example 21

If in doubt, argue merit principle (what you believe is the right thing to do).

The matter at issue in a VEOA appeal, however, is not whether a particular agency action is proper and should be sustained. Id.; *Villamarzo v. Environmental Protection Agency*, 92 M.S.P.R. 159, ¶ 5 (2002). VEOA gives the board no authority to adjudicate the merits of any agency action. Id. Instead, VEOA authorizes the Board to determine only whether an agency, in connection with the action that is the subject of an appeal, has violated a statutory or regulatory provision relating to veterans' preference.

This is where you must be creative because the agency will get creative and often downright nasty.

Case law example 22

Raise every issue you can.

"The appellant also asserted that the agency violated 5 U.S.C. §§ 3311 and 3320, as well as 5 C.F.R. § 302.202, by failing to properly credit his military experience and his two years of "experience in developing (sic) country." See IAF, Tabs 8, 28, 33. However, the administrative judge found that the appellant failed to raise this allegation in the complaint he had filed with the Department of Labor. Because the appellant failed to show that he exhausted this argument, the administrative judge dismissed this claim.

Pay close attention to this case law because it clearly explains that the Department of Labor's jurisdiction is plenary. If you fail to raise an issue, the MSPB will gladly dismiss your claim. This case tells me that your experience is a factor that may be considered as a rating and ranking issue. Be creative.

Case law example 23

Your veteran's preference rights do not always apply, so find a job announcement where they do apply.

This distinction is crucial, since the veteran's preference rules that must be followed in an open competitive examination do not apply to a merit promotion action. *Joseph v. Federal Trade Commission*, 103 M.S.P.R. 684, ¶¶ 12-13 (2006), aff'd, 505 F.3d 1380 (Fed. Cir. 2007); *Brandt v. Department of the Air Force*, 103 M.S.P.R. 671, ¶ 16 (2006).

This rarely occurs. There are not many positions you cannot apply for.

Case law example 24

The agency may be required to reconstruct its selection if you're not hired.

"He further found that the refiled appeal concerned whether the agency violated a statute or regulation relating to veterans' preference in the manner in which it conducted the reconstructed selection process, but that the appellant failed to file a complaint with DOL alleging that DFAS (a federal agency) committed such a violation when it reconstructed the hiring process." Basically, the veteran failed to file a new complaint when the veteran somehow discovered that the agency did not properly reconstruct the job announcement.

Case law example 25

This presents a good example of how applicants are ranked and rated.

In a traditional competitive examination, preference-eligible veterans have additional points added to their passing scores. 5 U.S.C. § 3309; 5 C.F.R. § 337.101(b). The names of applicants are entered onto registers, or lists of eligibles, in rank order, with preference eligibles ranked ahead of others with the same rating. See 5 U.S.C. § 3313; 5 C.F.R. § 332.401. The appointing authority must make a selection from the highest three eligible on the list, 5 U.S.C. § 3318(a), and must justify a decision to pass over a preference eligible in order to select a nonpreference eligible, 5 U.S.C. § 3318(b).

I suggest you do more research on Passover requirements.

Case law example 26

To establish exhaustion, the appellant must show that he provided the Department of Labor with a summary of the allegations forming the basis of his complaint so that Department of Labor can conduct an investigation. See *Burroughs v. Department of the Army*, 115 M.S.P.R. 656, ¶ 9, aff'd, 445 F. App'x 347 (Fed. Cir. 2011). The purpose of this requirement is to afford Department of Labor the opportunity to conduct an investigation that might lead to corrective action before involving the board in the case. See 5 U.S.C. § 3330a(b)-(c); Burroughs, 115 M.S.P.R. 656, ¶ 9.

Do not let the Department of Labor tell you that it has no enforcement power.

Case law example 27

If you're placed in the highest category, then you should not be passed over.

A preference eligible with a compensable service-connected disability of 10% or more must be listed in the highest quality category; within a category, preference eligible veterans are listed ahead of non-preference eligibles; and an agency may not select a non-preference eligible ahead of a preference eligible in the same category unless it seeks and receives approval for a passover. 5 U.S.C. § 3319.

Again, review your passover rights.

Appendix A

FAQs on Veterans Opportunity to Work to Hire Heroes Act of 2011

Q. What is the VOW to Hire Heroes Act of 2011?

A. The VOW (Veterans Opportunity to Work) To Hire Heroes Act of 2011 was signed into law by President Obama on November 22, 2011. It requires Federal agencies to treat active duty service members as veterans, disabled veterans and preference eligibles for purposes of an appointment in the competitive service.

Q. Why was VOW enacted?

A. Many service members begin their civilian job search prior to being discharged or released from active duty service and thus do not have a DD form 214, *Certificate of Release or Discharge from Active Duty,* when applying for Federal jobs. The VOW Act was enacted to ensure these individuals do not lose the opportunity to be considered for Federal service (and awarded their veterans' preference entitlements if applicable) despite not having a DD form 214 to submit along with their résumés.

Q. What type of documentation is an active duty service member required to furnish with a job application?

A. The VOW requires the active duty service member to furnish a "certification."

Q. What is a "certification?"

A. A "certification" is any written document from the armed forces that certifies the service member is expected to be discharged or released from active duty service in the armed forces under honorable conditions not later than 120 days after the date the certification is signed.

Q. What affect does this new provision have on how agencies process a pplications of eligible veterans?

A. Agencies are required to accept, process, and grant tentative veterans' preference to those active duty service members who submit a certification along with their job application materials.

Q. Should agencies automatically award veterans' preference to individuals eligible under the VOW Act upon receiving the veteran's job application?

A. No, agencies must grant service members' tentative veterans' preference but verify the individual meets the definition of 'preference eligible' under 5 U.S.C. 2108 prior to appointment.

Q. What should an agency do if the certification has expired, i.e., more than 120 days have lapsed since the date the certification was signed?

A. If the certification has expired; an agency must request other documentation (e.g., a copy of the DD form 214) that demonstrates the service member is a preference eligible per 5 U.S.C. 2108, before veterans' preference can be awarded.

Q. Does this new section 2108a of title 5 United States Code (U.S.C.) apply to the Excepted Service?

A. No. The provisions in title 5 U.S.C. 2108a apply only to applications for appointments in the competitive service.

Appendix B

Below is a list of the Occupational Series. This list is not complete. Visit www.usajobs.gov for complete list of position titles within each Occupational Series listed below. You may use the information listed be as a resource for Google purposes.

Occupational Series

- 0000-0099—Miscellaneous Occupations
- 0100-0199—Social Science, Psychology, and Welfare
- 0200-0299—Human Resources Management
- 0300-0399—General Administrative, Clerical, and Office Services
- 0400-0499—Biological Sciences
- 0500-0599—Accounting and Budget
- 0600-0699—Medical, Hospital, Dental, and Public Health
- 0700-0799—Veterinary Medical Science
- 0800-0899—Engineering and Architecture
- 0900-0999—Legal and Kindred
- 1000-1099—Information and Arts
- 1100-1199—Business and Industry
- 1200-1299—Copyright, Patent, and Trade-Mark
- 1300-1399—Physical Sciences
- 1400-1499—Library and Archives
- 1500-1599—Mathematics and Statistics
- 1600-1699—Equipment, Facilities, and Service
- 1700-1799—Education
- 1800-1899—Inspection, Investigation, Enforcement, and Compliance

- 1900-1999—Quality Assurance, Inspection and Grading
- 2000-2099—Supply
- 2100-2199—Transportation
- 2200-2299—Information Technology Management
  (The links above are linked to www.opm.gov. Click on them to access the series of choice.)

Appendix C

You may submit Form 1010 in either of two ways:

1. **Submitting a signed hard copy of Form 1010.** You may download **Form 1010** to your computer, complete the items on the form that are relevant to your claim, print the form, sign and date the form, and then either mail it, or fax it, or deliver it in person, to the following VETS office *only*:

    Veterans' Employment and Training Service
    U.S. Department of Labor
    ATTENTION: Form 1010
    61 Forsyth Street, S.W., Room 6T85
    Atlanta, Georgia 30303
    FAX: (404) 562-2313

    The Form 1010 information you enter after download is not being saved or collected from this Internet site; instead, you must print out the completed form and either mail it, or fax it, or deliver it in person, to the VETS address shown above.

2. **Submitting Form 1010 electronically via the Internet.** If you prefer to file Form 1010 electronically via the Internet instead of mailing a printed form, you can complete and submit the "On-line" version of Form 1010 at VETS 1010 Form On-line Submission website: https://vets1010.dol.gov/.

    By law, Veterans' Preference complaints must be received by VETS, in writing or via the VETS 1010 Form On-line Submission website, within 60 days of the date of the alleged veterans' preference violation or the complaint will be determined as "not timely", and closed without action.

Please read the Privacy Act statement and certification on page two of Form 1010 before signing and submitting the form.

Below are some brief instructions on filling out Form 1010. However, if questions arise that are not addressed here, please contact the nearest VETS office for assistance.

SPECIFIC INSTRUCTIONS

NOTE: These instructions are for persons filing Veterans' Preference claims only. If you are filing a USERRA complaint, please refer to the instructions in the USERRA Advisor.

Section I

Self-explanatory. Social Security number is optional, but desired.

Section II

For this section please use the branch of service that you were, are or will be in when the allegations that lead you to file this complaint occurred. For each question, answer to the best of your ability only the questions that apply to you. This information must eventually be supported with documentation in order for VETS to establish your eligibility under the law.

- **Question 8**—Fill in the branch of service you that you are, have been or will be a member of. May leave this question blank if filing a VP claim.
- **Question 9**—Fill in the specific information you have of your unit including name, address and phone number.
- **Question 10**—Fill in the dates that you served in, the date that you began your service, or the date that you will begin your service.

- **Question 11**—Fill in the appropriate bubble that best describes how you were discharged.

Section III

Please report the information of the employer(s) that your complaint involves. Do so accurately because this information will be used to establish a point of contact within the agency or company.

- **Question 12**—Fill in the name of your employer or the employer you are applying for.
- **Question 13**—Fill in the address.
- **Question 14**—
  1. Fill in the name and, if possible, title of whoever you are or have been in contact with regarding your position.
     (Often a HR specialist or supervisor)
  2. Fill in their phone number
- **Question 15**—Fill in the dates that you have been employed with this employer, the date that you started working for this employer, or the date you will start working for this employer.
- **Question 16**—Fill in no if you have not exceeded five cumulative years of uniformed service with this employer. Answer yes, and explain in the comment section below, if you have.
- **Question 17**—Fill in the name of any Union(s) that may represent you.
- **Question 18**—Fill in the title of the position you have, had or are applying to.

Section IV

Please use this section to detail some specifics of your complaint. Answer each question that applies to you as completely and accurately as you can.

- **Leave Question 19 blank.**—Question 19 is for USERRA complaints only.

If Claim Concerns Veterans' Preference in Federal Hiring

- **Question 20**—If you feel that your Veterans' Preference rights were violated regarding a position within a **Federal Agency**, please fill in the issue that best describes your complaint.
- **Leave Question 21 blank**. Question 21 is for USERRA complaints only.

If Claim Concerns Hiring, RIF, Promotion or Termination

- **Question 22**—Fill in the title of the position that relates to this complaint.
- **Leave Questions 23 through 24 blank.** Questions 23 through 24 are for USERRA complaints only.

If Claim Concerns Reemployment Following Service

- **Leave Questions 25 through 28 blank.** Questions 25 through 28 are for USERRA complaints only.
- **Question 29**—Fill in the name and title of the person who you applied for reemployment with.
- **Question 30**—Fill in yes and the date if you are reemployed or have been reinstated with your employer.
  a. If yes, fill in your position and pay rate.
  b. If no, fill in the date that your reemployment was denied and state the reason that was given.
  c. Fill in the name of who within your employer denied your reemployment.

<u>Comments</u>

Please write clearly and coherently why you are filing this claim. Detail what remedies (e.g., employment, reemployment rights, lost wages, and seniority benefits) you seek by filing this claim.

APPENDIX D

THE POWER OF A REQUEST FOR INFORMATION

The information listed below is an example of a Request for Information (RFI). Each RFI must be tailored to the issues relating to your veterans preference/mix motive claim, which should contain particular relevant information and evidence to prove that your preference rights/EEO rights were violated. Department of Labor investigators are not required to draft a RFI for each case that is going to be processed and investigated under the Veterans Employment Opportunity Act. Make sure that the RFI is included in the MSPB file when you file your corrective action claim. You may have to submit it yourself. You may want to assist your investigator by drafting the RFI yourself because the Department of Labor is busy and backlogged. You are the expert on the application you submitted. It is up to you to make it clear. Let this RFI be your guide. Make it count. The bottom line is that a strong RFI could save you thousands in discovery costs. Here's the best part: Once the federal agency responds to your RFI, it cannot change its story. You don't have to be formal. Use the examples in Appendix E.

Appendix E

Request for Information Example 1

(Submit this to the agency by email as soon as you believe your veterans right may have been violated. Remember you have to formally file with the US Merit System Protection Board within 60 days of the date you become aware of the actually violation. Maintain this as part of your record. If the responding agency does not provide this to you upon your informal request you still have the opportunity to get it later after you have formally filed.)

John Doe
555 Main Street
Fort Worth, TX 55555

(Federal Agency Here)
(Address Here)

Re: Request for Information

Dear Selecting Official:

1. Submit a complete copy of all certificates issued for job announcement 1234-56-122333.
2. Submit a list of all applicants selected for job announcement 1234-56-122333. Identify each by: (a) name, (b) race/sex/etc., (c) date of hire, (d) position, (e) department, and (f) veteran's preference status.
3. Submit a list of all employees selected during the period (provide date) to (provide date), for job announcement 1234-56-122333. Identify

each by (a) name, (b) race/sex/etc., (c) date of hire, and (d) veteran's preference code.

4. Submit the name of the selecting official for job announcement 1234-56-122333.

5. Submit a detailed statement explaining why I (your name here) was not selected for the position for job announcement 1234-56-122333.

6. Submit a copy of letter submitted to the Office of Personnel Management that proves the agency properly followed the passover procedures as required by all applicable laws.

7. If applicable, submit a detailed statement of the reason the why the selecting officials did not use the VEOA certificate of eligible.

8. If applicable, submit a detailed statement of the reason the why the selecting officials did not use the VRA certificate of eligible.

9. If applicable, submit a detailed reason explaining why I (your name here) was not within the top three of all applicable certificates of eligible.

Sincerely,

John Doe

APPENDIX F

REQUEST FOR INFORMATION EXAMPLE 2

If you applied for a job and you believe you were more qualified the questions below are a good example. The information below is a very powerful tool rarely used by investigators. Most attorneys will not take the time to draft a RFI so just do it yourself. Using this RFI will save you money in the long run. You're the master of your case because you know the contours of every situation that got you there. The earlier you take control, the more likely it is you will win your case. When using an RFI, be specific to the facts of your case. Doing an RFI during the investigative stage will not interfere with the official discovery phase. This advice is given because during the official discovery phase, the administrative judge will limit the amount of discovery you can get.

Request for Information

1. Provide the name, race, gender, amount veteran's preference, and contact information of each person who applied for the program support assistant position.

2. Provide the name, race, and gender of all applicants who had their names forwarded to the selecting official for consideration of the program support assistant position.

3. Provide the name, race, and gender of each person who was interviewed for the program support assistant position.

4. Provide the name, race, gender, and contact information of the last three employees who held the program support assistant position.

5. What information regarding each applicant was forwarded to the selecting official for the program support assistant position? Please explain what information was excluded, if any.

6. Who decided that the program support assistant position would be announced as a merit promotion only?

7. Under what authority does the agency have to create different certificates of eligibility (for example, reinstatement, transfer, reassignment, etc.)?

8. What factors were used to determine the program support assistant position would be announced as merit promotion only?

9. Why was the program support assistant position not open to the public?

10. What is the promotion potential for the program support assistant position?

11. Who created the announcement for the program support assistant position and advertised it?

12. Where was the announcement for the program support assistant posted?

13. Did anyone receive advance notice that the program support assistant was going to be announced?

14. Was the announcement for the program support assistant position posted on USAJobs.gov? If no, why? If yes, why?

15. For the program support assistant position, who decided to create several different certificates under the merit promotion announcement?

16. For the program support assistant position, why were several different certificates created under the merit promotion announcement?

17. For the program support assistant position, when several certificates were created, did the person who created the several certificates know that Ms. Susan Joe would not be eligible under any of those certificates?

18. For the program support assistant position, did the announcement notify applicants of who may apply (for example, reassignment, laterals, reinstatement, etc.)? If no, why? If yes, why?

19. For the program support assistant position, when was it decided that the person who was going to be selected would require extensive budget experience?

20. Were all applicants notified that extensive experience in budgeting would be part of the determining factor in the selection process for the program support assistant position? If no, why? If yes, how were they notified and when?

21. For the program support assistant position, was extensive budget experience a determining factor in the selection decision for the last three employees who have held the position? If no, why? If yes, why?

22. Why would a program support assistant position require extensive budget experience?

23. In the course of a work day, what amount of time is spent by the program support assistant in education services doing budget operation?

24. What actual duties, to date, relate to budgeting are performed by the program support assistant position?

25. What performance rating did the previous employee who performed the duties for the program support assistant position receive?

26. Are employees rated on their performance in budgeting as part of their formal duties for the program support assistant position? If yes, what are the determining factors used to rate performance as it relates to budgeting?

27. For the program support assistant position, how did the rater or selection official determine what was extensive experience in budgeting? For example, was the decision based on the number of years of experience in budgeting or the amount of money handled in budgeting? Whatever your answer, did all applicants receive prior notice of what the process would be to determine how qualifying budget experience would be more or less qualifying?

28. Did Susan Joe's experience for the program support assistant position indicate she was the assistant superintendent of education and training, which included experience in budgeting and allocation?

29. Who decided for the program support assistant position would require extensive budget experience?

30. Why was the announcement for the program support assistant position not advertised with the requirement of extensive budget experience?

31. Do OPM guidelines for the program support assistant position require extensive budget experience? If no, then why did the selection decision in this instance matter require extensive budget experience?

32. When the certificates of eligible were created for the program support assistant position, how were applicants ranked? For example, were applicants ranked qualified, well-qualified, or (best) highly qualified?

33. Provide a copy of the ranking of each applicant for the program support assistant position.

34. Did any applicants from outside the New York VA apply for the program support assistant position? If yes, how were they notified of the available position?

35. What factors were used to determine which certificate of eligible list would be used to select the program support assistant?

36. Did any employee receive notification of the job announcement outside of the means the announcement was posted for all employees? For example, did Susan Hall or anyone from the human resources office fax, email, or verbally notify an employee the announcement had been made? If yes, who received this type of notification and why?

37. Who determined there was a need for the program support assistant position in the education department? What was the need based on?

Request for Information (Part II)

(These questions are intended for whomever directly caused you harm.)

1. Before charging Susan Joe with AWOL, did you confer with Joe Smith about whether Susan Joe notified him of her absence? If yes, what did Joe Smith tell you about the circumstances of Susan Joe's absence? If you did not confer with Joe Smith, then why?

2. Did you conduct an investigation prior to charging Susan Joe of AWOL, or did you summarily charge her with AWOL without relevant facts?

3. Did Joe Smith confer with you on August 24, 2001, regarding Susan Joe's absence? If yes, what was the discussion about?

4. Did you confer with Joel Elliot about whether Susan Joe had contacted him regarding her absence prior to charging Susan Joe with AWOL? If no, then why? If yes, then why?

5. What factors, if any, did you consider before charging Susan Joe with AWOL?

6. On a Report of Contact form, Joel Elliot stated that he was contacted by Susan Joe on August 23, 2001, at 8:25 a.m., regarding her involvement in a "major traffic tie up." Did you confer with Mr. Elliot before charging Susan Joe with AWOL? If no, why not? If yes, what did Mr. Elliot convey to you that led you to charge Susan Joe with AWOL?

7. Did Susan Joe send you an email conveying her interest in the interim supervisor position? If yes, provide a copy.

8. Did Susan Joe state or express any of her concerns in the presence of Brad Mills with then-union representative Mary George that she did not have any interest in the interim supervisor position?

9. Ms. Mary George has stated that she was present when Susan Joe expressed her concern of not wanting to be placed in the interim

supervisor position. Please explain why Ms. George's statements are inconsistent with Brad Mills statements because George is stating that Susan Joe made it clear to Curry that she did not want to be in the interim supervisor position.

10. Why was it decided that Susan Joe would be the first interim supervisor? What were the determining factors?

11. What factors were used to determine Susan Joe performance was no longer exceptional? For example, did Susan Joe performance worsen, causing you to rate her to fully successfully and no longer exceptional?

12. What factors of performance did Joel Esquivel fail to consider when he rated Susan Joe's performance as exceptional?

13. Did the performance rating criteria change that warranted a change in Susan Joe's performance from exceptional to fully successful?

14. When you considered placing Susan Joe in the interim supervisor position, did you consider that her performance had fallen from exceptional to fully successful? If yes, why? If no, why?

15. Did Susan Joe say in the presence of then-union representative Mary George during a mediation that she would resign if she were forced to work under your direct supervision?

16. Susan Joe states that she provided you with a copy of her self-assessment prior to you rating her performance. Did you consider the self-assessment your evaluation? If no, explain why.

17. During the course of your career with the Department of Veterans Affairs or any other federal agency, have you been charged or accused of discrimination pursuant to Title VII of the 1964 Civil Rights Act? If yes, explain the circumstances of each complaint against you.

APPENDIX G

FAQs

I added this section because I wanted a preference eligible to understand the concept of what you are dealing with and how your rights relate to many aspects of seeking redress under Title VII of the 1964 Civil Rights Act in light of a veteran's preference claim. You should take the position that your rights are unlimited and they cross many avenues. For example, let's say that you file a complaint with the Department of Labor for a veteran's preference violation and that you also believe that you were not selected for a position because of your disability. You then have the right to file a complaint under Title VII for disability discrimination with the agencies equal employment officer. Keep in mind that you can also file a complaint with the Merit System Protection Board to preserve your rights to the Title VII claim. Essentially, then, you will be filing three claims: a claim with the Department of Labor, a claim with the agency's EEO office, and a claim with the Merit System Protection Board. The FAQs below are questions received from people that relate to policy and procedures of the EEOC. The commission's policies and procedures govern federal agencies. Remember that when you file a charge of discrimination against a federal agency, you must contact the agency's EEO officer. Please do not be confused—you do not file a charge of discrimination with the private sector EEOC office against a federal agency. Below you will notice that the question refer to the EEOC. That's because federal agencies' EEO processes are the same. Follow these FAQs, and apply them to any form that relates to your veteran's preference and Title VII rights.

FAQs Related to EEO Matters

1. What is the time limitation for filing a charge of discrimination under Title VII against a federal agency?

    Answer: You have forty-five days from the date you become aware of the harm.

2. Once I file, how many days does the federal agency have to answer my complaint?

    Answer: A federal agency has thirty days to answer your complaint. It may be extended up to sixty days with your permission.

3. When it has been determined that conciliation efforts have been unsuccessful and that further efforts would be futile or nonproductive, must the charging party and respondent be notified? (This applies to private sector complaints. Note that a complaint of discrimination against a federal agency is not considered a private sector complaint.)

    Answer: Yes.

4. Does the EEOC have to keep the charging party informed about the conciliation discussions?

    Answer: Yes.

5. Does the EEOC have to engage in conciliation discussions with respondents when it issues reasonable cause determinations?

    Answer: Yes. This applies only to private sector complaints. The federal sector does not issue reasonable cause findings. Federal agencies do not issue reasonable cause findings. They are only required to conduct neutral fact-finding investigations.

6. What happens to a charging party or respondent who provides false evidence during the course of an investigation?

Answer: Title 18 U.S.C. § 1001 of the federal criminal code prohibits the submission of false information during an official investigation. If you don't have the evidence to support the allegation(s), do not submit false evidence. The same holds true for respondent.

7. What policies or procedures give outside applicants and government employees the opportunity to file charges of discrimination against the government?

   Answer: Each federal agency is required to have a director of EEO who is responsible for the implementation of a continuing affirmative employment program to promote equal employment and to identify and eliminate discriminatory practices and policies. In addition, each agency must develop policies, procedures, and guidance relating to the processing of employment discrimination complaints governed by the Commission's Regulations in 29 C.F.R. Par 1614. These policies and procedures can be found at www.eeoc.gov/federal/md110/md.html.

8. Can an applicant who applied for a position with the federal government who is not selected file a charge of discrimination with the EEOC?

   Answer: No. The applicant must contact the agency and get the name of an EEO counselor to begin the precomplaint counseling within forty-five days of the date of alleged discrimination. Federal employees are governed by the same procedures.

9. Does the Department of Labor's Office of Federal Contract and Compliance (OFCCP) enforce Section 503 0f the Rehabilitation Act of 1973 and Vietnam Era Veterans' Readjustment Assistants Act of 1974?

   Answer: Yes. Section 503 of the Rehabilitation Act gives veterans the right to file with OFCCP.

10. Where does a disabled veteran go to file a charge of discrimination if he/she was not hired or promoted for a job?

Answer: The Department of Labor (under the Veterans Employment Opportunity Act). The disabled veteran has sixty days in most cases.

11. What will happens to an employer that doesn't comply?

Answer: The employer can be fined up to $17,000 for each offense per location.

12. What posters must employers to display for employees and applicants to see?

Answer: Fair Labor Standards Act (minimum wage) poster, the Family and Medical Leave poster; USERRA notice, Equal Employment Opportunity poster, Occupational Safety and Health (OSHA) poster, and the Polygraph Protection poster.

13. What federal agency has authority of enforcing the Family Medical Leave Act of 1993?

Answer: The Department of Labor.

14. Can a charging party with an arrest and conviction record file a charge of discrimination with the EEOC?

Answer: Yes. Review the EEOC's policy on arrest and criminal records at www.eeoc.gov. Veterans with arrest records can file a complaint with the Merit System Protection Board for suitability determination.

15. Must a charging party file an internal complaint with human resources before coming to the EEOC and filing a charge of discrimination?

Answer: No.

16. Can an employer give a charging party a negative reference after he/she has been terminated and filed a charge of discrimination?

Answer: No. In furnishing oral or written references concerning charging party, the employer may mention only the nature and duration of charging party's employment.

17. What should a charging party do after making several attempts to an investigator about the status of his or her case?

Answer: Charging parties should make no more than four telephone calls to an investigator about the status of a case. Log the dates and times, why each call was made, and make sure a message is left with the best time to return the call. If the investigator fails to return calls, send a certified letter to the investigator and copy the district director. If no response is received, write your congressional representative.

18. What is the best way to have back pay calculated?

Answer: By quarters. The information listed below describes the procedures: what were you making at the place of employment when the discrimination occurred (hourly rate or base salary); what you actually made or would have been making by using reasonable credited earnings; add any loss from previous quarters (carry over loss) to quarter loss; calculate interest for that quarter on total loses; and add interest using the current IRS interest rate.

19. What documents are excluded from the investigative file?

Answer: Confidential witness information; cover sheets on commission decisions; investigator's notes; and supervisory memorandums that reveal recommendations, proposals, strategy, or deliberative processing actions of a charge; and all memorandums and notes from the regional attorney, the Office of General Counsel, legal counsel, or the Department of Justice; all information identifying other respondents; and all reports that EEOC request other respondents to submit. The EEO-1 Report on the respondent that a charging party has filed a charge against and the document can be made available upon request. Always make a request that the Log of Investigation Settlement Action EEOC Form 159 is included when the file is receive investigator must be on this form.

20. Can a charging party request a copy of the investigative file?

Answer: Yes. Some EEOC offices will require charging parties to complete and sign an EEOC form 157 agreement of nondisclosure. The investigator will be sent to a company that that EEOC has a contract with. The charging party will be required to pay for copying fees.

21. What is a position statement?

Answer: The respondent's position statement is nothing more than telling its side of the story regarding the allegation(s) raised in the charge. The EEOC has dismissed numerous cases without respondent's position statement. Do not let the EEOC dismiss your case without your input.

22. What is the purpose of predetermination interviews (PDI)?

Answer: The EEOC's Compliance Manuel Procedures Volume I Section 27 states a PDI should held with respondent in cause cases and with charging party and in no cause cases when sufficient evidence has been obtained to support a proposed determination. There are expectations regarding these procedures. The purposes of the PDI are to inform the respondent and charging parties of the proposed finding and give them a final opportunity to provide additional information in the case. Charging parties should never have a PDI with an investigator without having a copy of respondent's position statement. Ask the investigator for a copy of the respondent's position statement. If facts are disputed in the position statement, submit them in writing with the evidence and send the information to the investigator by certified mail. The EEOC is allowing investigators to dismiss cases without giving charging parties PDIs.

23. What should an employer know about the EEOC?

Answer: The employer should that the EEOC is an independent federal agency created by Congress in 1964 to eradicate employment discrimination. The EEOC has the authority to receive, initiate, and investigate charges of discrimination filed against employers who have a statutory minimum number of employees. Its role in an investigation is to fairly and accurately evaluate the charge allegations of all the evidence obtained. This information can be found at www.eeoc.gov/employers/investigations.html.

24. When an aggrieved person participates in the EEOC's mediation program to resolve a charge of discrimination, will he or she likely be satisfied with the settlement results?

Answer: The EEOC's mediation program is just a con and shell game played on the charging party and respondent. In most cases, the employer is going to offer the charging party as little as possible to resolve the case. It might be different if you can afford to hire an attorney to participate in the mediation. However, if you can't afford an attorney, call a civil rights organization and see if one of its representatives will attend the mediation. The only real advantage of mediation is to see how serious the respondent is about resolving the case. Don't disclosed evidence and/or names of witnesses during the mediation.

25. Can an aggrieved person(s) elect not to participate in the EEOC's mediation program?

Answer: Yes.

26. Can an aggrieved person(s) who filed a charge of discrimination call and inquire about the status of his or her charge?

Answer: Yes. Aggrieved individuals who have filed a charge should wait approximately ninety days before making a call. Ask whether the employer has submitted a statement of position. If so, ask for a copy of it. Some of the EEOC offices will require the charging party to complete and sign EEOC's form 157 agreement of nondisclosure, while others will just require you to write a letter. Only request a copy of the employer's statement of position at the time. You can get a copy of the investigative file at a later date. Also ask the investigator how your charge was classified. (If the charge was initially categorized as category C, ask the investigator why you were not promptly informed.)

27. In what category are the majority of charges filed by African American and other minorities placed?

Answer: Category C. The agency's IMS Reports are evidence to support this fact.

28. What can cause a charge to be dismissed?

Answer: Nonjurisdictional charges and those failing to state a claim (dismiss under 29 C.F.R. § 1601.18); charges unsupported by any direct or circumstantial evidence of discrimination and the charging party was in a position to have access to such evidence (dismiss under 29 C.F.R. § 1601.19 and §§ 1601.15[b] and 1601.18[b]); self-defeating charges (dismiss under 29 C.F.R. § 1601.19); charges where the allegations are not credible, including cases filed by repetitive charge filers where, based on the large number of charges, the charging party is not credible (dismiss under 29 CF.R. § 1601.19); and ADA charges filed more than 180/300 days after the date of violation.

29. Are there limitations for monetary relief under the ADEA and EPA?

Answer: Yes. The ADEA and EPA statues of limitations bar recovery of relief for actions that occur more than two years before lawsuit if filed by an aggrieved person(s) or EEOC (three years in case of willful violation at the time the violation occurred.)

30. How are charges classified under the EEOC's Priority Charge Handling Procedures (PCHP)?

Answer: The Priority Categorization System classifies charges into the following categories:

- Category A: Enforcement plan/potential cause charges. This first category includes charges that fall within the national or local enforcement plan and other charges where further investigation will probably result in a cause finding. Charges should also be classified as category A if irreparable harm will result unless processing is expedited.

- Category B: Charges requiring additional information. Many of these charges will initially appear to have some merit but will require additional evidence to determine whether continued investigation is likely to result in a cause finding. In addition, in other cases, it will simply not be possible to make a judgment regarding the merits of the charge at charge receipt. In these cases, additional investigation will be needed, as resources permit, to determine whether these charges should be moved into category A and given priority status or moved into category C and dismissed. Category B charges may be placed in suspension where the charging party has filed suit based on the issues raised in the charge.

- Category C: Charges suitable for dismissal. A charge placed in this category can be dismissed when the office has sufficient evidence from which it is not likely that further investigation will result in a cause finding.

31. Does the EEOC have a time limitation to notify an employer after a charge has been filed by an aggrieved person(s)?

Answer: Yes. Aggrieved person(s) should be informed at the intake process that the employer will be notified within ten days of receipt of the charge. The identity of the aggrieved person(s) who filed the charge will also be revealed. The employer will receive EEOC form 131 (Notice of Charge of Discrimination), which will either request a position statement or request for information. The employer is given thirty days to respond.

32. Can a female aggrieved person(s) file an EPA charge without a Title VII charge?

Answer: Yes. In an EPA charge of discrimination, an aggrieved person(s) must be very careful. To prevail, an individual must have equal skill, effort, and responsibility to similarly situated males working at the employer's facilities. If one of the aforementioned factors is missing, though, it will be difficult to file a charge under the EPA.

33. What are the limitations on the amount of damages that a charging party can recover?

Answer: Damages are based on the size (number of employees) of the employer. The limitations are stated as follows: 15 to 100 employees, $50,000; 101 to 200 employees, $100,000; 201 to 500 employees, $200,000; and 501 employees or more, $300,000.

34. Can aggrieved person(s) recover damages under Section 1981(A) (b)?

Answer: Yes. Section 1981(A) (b) sets limitations on certain damages that aggrieved person(s) may recover. For example, it specifies that punitive damages are available only if the aggrieved person can demonstrate that respondent engaged in discrimination "with malice and reckless indifference to the federally protected rights of an aggrieved person." It also provides that punitive damages are not available against governmental entity or political subdivisions. In addition, it reiterates that compensatory damages do not include any relief authorized under § 706 (g) of Title VII. It also provides a limitation on the sum of punitive damages and compensatory damages for "future pecuniary losses, emotional pain, suffering, inconvenience, mental anguish, loss of enjoyment of life, and other non-pecuniary losses." Aggrieved person(s) who have filed charges of discrimination should go to their doctors and other medical professionals and seek medical treatment as soon as possible. If you do not have insurance, go anyway and keep a record of the doctors who turn you away.

35. What are the advantages of filing a lawsuit under Section 1981?

Answer: Section 1981 imposes no limitations like Title VII of fifteen or more employees. A charging party cannot sue employees under Title VII. However, under Section 1981, there is no limit on the number of employees, and they can be sued. Respondents get frightened when they see a lawsuit with a Section 1981. The statute of limitations for filing a Section 1981 is four years. An aggrieved person can go right to court under a Section 1981 without going to EEOC and filing a charge of discrimination.

36. Can a Section 1981 include a pattern or practice for quid pro quo claims?

Answer: No. Race and retaliation can be brought only under Section 1981.

37. Is there a back pay limit under Title VII?

Answer: Yes. Back pay may be obtained under Title VII for a period of up to two years before the filing of a charge, so long as the charge itself is timely filed pursuant to 29 C.F.R. § 1626.7 (d) (1) and § 605.7.

38. Can aggrieved person(s) file concurrent ADEA and EPA complaints?

Answer: Yes. The EEOC will not process ADEA or EPA complaints that do not allege violations affecting any aggrieved person within two years (three years in cases of willful violations) of the date of the complaint.

39. Can aggrieved person(s) file concurrent charges (a Title VII and an ADEA complaint) with the EEOC?

Answer: Yes. There is a 180-day limit on the filing of a Title VII and ADEA charge. ADEA charges can be filed for EEOC processing within two years (three years in cases of willful violations of the alleged violation pursuant to 29 C.F.R. § 1626.7 [a]). When an ADEA charge is filed in a jurisdiction with a state agency, the time limit is generally 300 days or within thirty days of receipt of notice of the agency's action, whichever occurs first (see §1626.7 [b]). The EEOC may bring an action within the aforementioned two—or three-year time limits on its own if the charge was not timely filed.

40. Why is it important for EEOC investigators to conduct onsite investigations?

Answer: Onsite investigations should be conducted in cases classified in category A and C under EEOC's Priority Charge Handling Procedures (PCHP). Investigators have the opportunity to interview witnesses; tour the respondent's facility; and examine, copy, or transcribe records.

41. How much information should be put in a charge of discrimination?

Answer: EEOC offices are allowing investigators to put too must information in charges. Don't let investigators name your witnesses in the charge. Investigators take notes during the intake processing of a charge. However, on numerous occasions, these notes get lost. Request that the investigator transpose the notes into an affidavit for your signature and give you a copy. Always read the charge and affidavit very carefully before leaving the office to make sure that all of the allegations were listed.

Example: On January December 12, 2010, I was denied a promotion to the position of director of engineering. I have over thirty years of experience in my field, and I have worked in fifteen different countries on large engineering projects. I have received numerous awards for my job performance. Paul Smith, a white male, age 25, and with less experience and/or education, was selected for the position. On December 15, 2010, I filed an internal complaint with the human resources, but nothing was resolved. On December 29, 2010, I was terminated. I believe that I have been discriminated on the basis of race (Black), age (52), and retaliated against in violation of Title VII of the Civil Rights Act of 1964, as amended. I also believe that I have been discrimination against because of my age in violation of the Age Discrimination in Employment Act of 1967.

42. Is it wise to complete an intake questionnaire in the intake area at an EEOC office?

Answer: No. Remember this is the very first step of the investigation. There are too many distractions taking place with other aggrieved person(s) waiting to file charges of discrimination. They too are likely talking about what happened to them. There have been numerous times that aggrieved person(s) have omitted timely allegations. Take the intake questionnaire home and complete it. It will ask you to do the following: Describe the harm or employer action for which you are filing a complaint. Include the names and job titles of all those involved and the dates you were harmed. There is not enough room if you make more than one allegation. Therefore, draft a detail synopsis and say see attached. Make a copy of the intake questionnaire and synopsis for your record. Make sure that you list all witnesses. All testimony must be taken under oath before an investigator and/or officer that has the authority to administer the oaths to witnesses who is personally responsible for the recording.

43. Must an aggrieved person(s) complete an EEOC form 283 intake questionnaire before being seen by an investigator?

Answer: Yes. All aggrieved person(s) who visit an EEOC office must complete an intake questionnaire before being seen by an investigator. However, if the aggrieved person(s) has an attorney, he or she can get a copy of the intake questionnaire and give it to the attorney to complete and give it to the persons wanting to file a charge of discrimination.

44. Does the EEOC maintain a retention file for telephone or mail-in charges of discrimination?

Answer: Yes. Most EEOC offices maintain a sixty-day retention file organized by month of receipt of the charges/complaints filed alphabetically by the aggrieved person(s) name. Before disposal of any potential charge/complaint contained in the sixty-day file, a review of the charge/complaint must be made to ensure that any matter evidencing sufficient information warrant commission action (for example, a commissioner charge or a directed Equal Pay Act [EPA] or Age Discrimination in Employment Act [ADEA). Under the EEOC's Priority Charge Handling Procedures (PCHP), charges/complaints are maintained for ninety days before the charge inquiry is automatically closed. The charges or complaints are now monitored by EEOC's Integrated Mission System Report (IMS).

45. Can an aggrieved person(s) file a charge of discrimination by telephone with an EEOC office?

Answer: Yes. When a person lives outside the normal commuting area, the charge/complaint can be taken by telephone and mailed to the charging party or complainant for verification and signature. However, local charging parties or complainants should be encouraged to visit the office for an intake interview.

46. What happens to a case where EEOC has issued a reasonable cause determination and conciliation has failed?

Answer: If the reasonable cause determination is made to a private employer and conciliation efforts fail to resolve the case, the EEOC can make a decision depending on its workload to litigate the case. If not, it can issue the charging party a notice of right to sue so that he/she can file a lawsuit. In cases where a reasonable cause has been made against public, state, and local governments and conciliation efforts fail, the case must be sent to the Department of Justice to litigate.

Charging parties, please don't place any hope in the Department of Justice engaging in litigation on your case. If it happens, it will be a miracle. If the Justice Department decides not to litigate the case, it will issue a notice of right to sue to charging party.

47. Can a respondent file a petition to revoke a subpoena?

Answer: Yes. Respondents will petition to revoke a subpoena merely to delay an investigation. The EEOC must act on the petitions within established time frames (eight calendar days from receipt of the subpoena). The petition package will be distributed to the commission on a seventy-two-hour notice and hold consideration procedure. This is why the EEOC does not like to issue subpoenas if it can avoid because it might have to seek court enforcement.

48. Does the EEOC have subpoena authority?

Answer: Yes. In the event it is necessary to enforce a request for information against a respondent who refuses to cooperate, the EEOC has subpoena authority pursuant to § 1601.16 of EEOC's procedural regulations. District directors have the authority to sign and issue a subpoena. Investigators have no excuses of respondents not responding to requests for information and/or providing a position statement. No cases should be dismissed with respondent submitting a position statement.

49. What is the format and content of a fact finding conference?

Answer: The format and content are as follows.

The investigator will first introduce himself or herself and charging party. If respondent has brought additional evidence to the conference, it should be received by the investigator who should give a brief description of each type of document presented, so that the charging party is aware of the type of evidence presented to the investigator by the respondent. The investigator should explain that any additional evidence submitted during the conference will be analyzed. After conducting the preliminaries, the investigator should review the fact-finding conference process to ensure that all parties understand that

- Notes of the conference are being taken.
- If counsel for respondent and/or charging party is present, he or she will be limited to an advisory role and will not be permitted to speak for the client or to cross-examine.
- Each unresolved allegation of the charge will be closely examined and fully discussed. Ample time will be allowed to the charging party to explain and support each allegation and to the respondent to present and defend its position.
- Neither the charging party nor the respondent is permitted to bring a recording device into the conference.
- The EEOC has the authority to hold a fact-finding conference pursuant to § 1601.25 (c) and § 1626.15 (a) of EEOC's procedural regulations.

50. What is a fact-finding conference?

Answer: The fact-finding conference is an informal investigative technique rather than an adversarial proceeding. This procedure has always been available for investigators to use, but many don't take advantage of it to resolve cases.

51. How do the rapid processing procedures work?

Answer: Fact-finding conferences and informal settlements are part of the rapid-processing procedures. Investigators are required to draft an investigative plan (IP) and request for information (RFI), which should be tailored to address the issues directly affecting the charging party. Example, a fifty-year-old black applicant with three degrees in engineering and twenty-five years of experience applies on four different occasions to become director of the department but is not selected for the position. Respondent promotes a white male, age twenty-five with five years of experience, with only one degree in the same field. The RFI, Request for Position Statement, and copy of the charge must be sent with EEOC's form 131, Notice of Charge of Discrimination, to respondent. Settlement offers must be held in abeyance until after the investigator has received a response from the respondent. While waiting receipt of respondent's statement and response to the RFI, the investigator should interview charging party's witnesses. (Settlement offers should be held in abeyance until the RFI data and/or position statement has been received and analyzed.)

52. Does the EEOC have rapid-processing procedures in place to resolve cases?

Answer: Yes. Charges suitable for rapid processing from the intake unit can be processed under the rapid-processing procedures.

53. Can the EEOC file temporary or preliminary relief for charging parties or complainants?

Answer: Yes. In cases where retaliation is causing irreparable harm because an aggrieved person has filed a charge of discrimination against a respondent, the EEOC can file for temporary or preliminary relief. (Note to charging parties or complainants, if you are experiencing any type of retaliation after filing a charge of discrimination or providing testimony in a case, it is extremely important that you immediately contact the EEOC office where you filed your charge.) Most often, retaliation stems from the filing of a charge or complaint. The EEOC by law is required to take immediate legal action against the respondent.

54. Does a dismissal of a charge apply to charging parties or complainants who are deceased?

Answer: No. If the charging party or complainant dies, the above does not apply (If there are no other potentially aggrieved persons for whom EEOC would seek relief, the legal unit must determine whether a cause of action under state law survives the party and who inherits the rights and interest arising out of the charge.) (It is extremely important for charging parties and complainant to have an updated will for this purpose.)

55. What is the distinction between Title VII and ADEA and EPA dismissals?

Answer: Title VII requires that persons filing charges or those who file charges on behalf of others must sue within ninety days following receipt of notice of dismissal of the charging parties' right to sue. The ADEA and EPA don't contain this provision.

56. What happens when an employer files bankruptcy and is taken over by a successor?

Answer: It is not necessary for a charging party filing a charge or complaint that has been taken over by another company to file a separate charge against the successor company. A company that has assumed the personnel and primary business of a respondent is a successor company and assumes any charges filed against the original company. If the company is not a successor company and takes over the business property but makes a different product, a separate charge or compliant must be taken for each company if both are parties to the matters being aggrieved.

57. Can a charge be amended after it has been filed?

Answer: Yes. An amended charge is to cure a technical deficiency (the date of the most recent date of discrimination or to correct or add the respondent's correct address) or to add allegations that are like and related to the existing charge. If the amendment is made in a unit other than an intake unit, the amended charge should be taken by the investigator who was assigned the charge. If there are minor amendments that occur at the fact-finding conference, they should be added to the existing charge and initialed by the charging party.

58. Can an aggrieved person who files a charge, and if things become sensitive, is it possible that he or she could request another person of the same race or sex to process the charge?

Answer: Yes. When it becomes apparent that a potential aggrieved person is complaining about a sensitive incident of alleged sexual harassment or racial remarks, but is embarrassed or reluctant to discuss the matter with an intake investigator of the opposite sex, he/she should be given the option to talk to an investigator of the same race or sex.

59. Does the EEOC have a policy to deal with confidentiality for third-party charges and ADEA/EPA complaints?

Answer: Yes. The EEOC's policy is to not disclose the identity of aggrieved persons on whose behalf a Title VII or ADEA charge is filed or the identity of ADEA/EPA complaints. Every effort will be made to ensure that their identity will not be disclosed, unless required in a court action or prior written consent. Even though the person has requested confidentially, he or she may later permit the EEOC to use his/her name in a negotiated settlement or conciliation efforts.

60. When an ADEA complaint has only one identifiable aggrieved person and more than three years have passed since the date of the alleged violation, can the case be dismissed?

Answer: Yes. Under the ADEA, charges or complaints can be filed within two years in the case of willful violations. However, the EEOC will not process complaints when the alleged violation does not fall within the above time frames.

61. Will a charging party receive any counseling regarding a potential class charge?

Answer: Yes. Counseling should be given to a charging party with a potential class charge when the charge is based on an acknowledged respondent policy.

62. If a potential charging party comes to an EEOC field office to file a charge and has a Title VII, ADEA, ADA, or EPA claim, but lacks sufficient information to begin the intake process, can a charge be taken or will the person be required to wait until he or she returns to the office with the necessary information?

Answer: No. A charge should always be taken from a walk in with a valid claim regarding the aforementioned federal antidiscrimination laws, even if further information must be obtained before the investigation can continue.

63. Can a VEOA charge be amended after it has been filed?

Answer: Yes. An amended charge is to cure a technical deficiency (the date of the most recent date of a violation or to correct or add the respondent's correct address) or to add allegations that are like and related to the existing charge. If there are minor amendments that occur at the fact-finding conference, they should be added to the existing charge and initialed by the charging party.

APPENDIX H

EXAMPLE MOTION FOR SUMMARY JUDGMENT

Agencies will file motions for summary judgment before you can develop your facts. Below is an example of an opposition that I drafted that overwhelmed the defendant. Keep in mind that there is a twenty-page limitation in most federal district courts. Contact the court where you plan to file and get the local rules. This is not so hard that you shouldn't feel like you can do it. Simply follow the example that follows.

Jane Doe   Judge Seehemright
Plaintiff Pro Per
55555 N. W. Street
Mesa AZ 55555
555-555-555
fetjustice@aol.com

UNITED STATES DISTRICT COURT
DISTRICT OF ARIZONA

	Case No. (Court will assign Case No.)
Jane Doe, a married women	Opposition to Summary Judgment
v.	
XYZ Company	

COMES NOW Plaintiff, Jane Doe, pro se and hereby oppose the Motion For Summary Judgment filed by Defendant XYZ Company on the grounds that there are numerous material facts in dispute and that judgment is not allowed as a matter of law. Said Opposition is based on the attached Memorandum of Points and Authorities, Affidavits, Exhibits, and all pleadings on file with the Court in this matter.

I. MEMORANDUM OF POINT AND AUTHORITIES
INTRODUCTION

Plaintiff Jane Doe is an Mexican American female with a graduate degree in Business Administration and an undergraduate degree in Business Technology residing in Mesa, Arizona. Her education is unique in that she has not been able to obtain another job in the field of occupation in which she desires. Her inability to obtain a job in her field of choice is not the result of any court order but rather a conviction of a misdemeanor crime that was imposed by the Court just after her employment with Defendant XYZ Company and is the direct and proximate result of unlawful acts of Defendant. How this occurred is a story of discrimination and dishonesty that the Plaintiff will describe to this court setting forth in detail how the Defendant and their counsel have misstated the facts and the laws. Contrary to the Defendant's statement that "no material facts are disputed," numerous material facts are in dispute and numerous facts were not disclosed by Defendant XYZ Company in its Motion for Summary Judgment. The Defendant's citation to the Faragher-Ellerth affirmative defense shows the absurdity of its position and lack of support. False representations may work for the Defendant when no one is around but should not be used in a federal courtroom.

Since the date of the discriminatory treatment and up to the present, the Defendant has been engaged in retaliation against Jane Doe which has caused her to work mediocre jobs she is more than qualified to work.

II. STATEMENT OF FACTS

Defendant XYZ Company has asserted that no material facts are in dispute. Based on that statement, any material fact that actually supports plaintiff's position is not then disputed by the defendants. Listed below are material facts that are in support of the Plaintiff's claim thereby precluding summary judgment in favor of the Defendant.

Plaintiff Jane Doe was rehired with XYZ Company in 2003 to work as a business manager and promoted to a supervisory business manager in June 2005 and was constructively discharge in June 2007.

After Plaintiff was promoted to supervisory business manager, she was sexually harassed by Defendant XYZ Company employee John Doe (EXHIBIT 12 EEOC DETERMINATION LETTER and/or SEE file and XYZ Company reason for terminating John Doe, EXHIBIT 10) and subjected to discrete acts of retaliation and harassment that clearly were connected to the genesis of her sexual harassment complaint.

While serving as a supervisory business manager based in the southwestern district office, Jane Doe attempted to constructively discharge on two different occasions but was discouraged with what later turned out to be lies (offered another position within the department) (EXHIBIT D, p. 7 and Exhibit F, p.12, p. 23 in Declaration).

Plaintiff was told on the day of her June 2007 constructive discharge notice that someone filed a complaint against her two months prior (EXHIBIT O, p. 33, EXHIBIT W, p. 48 in Declaration, SEE EMAIL). However, the Plaintiff never received notice and fair warning of the allegations that would have allowed her the ability to overcome the (reassignment) administrative transfer.

The Plaintiff's June 2007 constructive discharge lends to Defendant XYZ Company subjecting her to an unlawful administrative transfer. The Plaintiff was denied her administrative due process rights that would have entitled her to a two-week notification and/or an administration hearing. (EXHIBIT 1, see Declaration).

The Plaintiff later reapplied for employment with XYZ Company after the constructive discharge but was met by a no rehire policy because she failed to live out her two-week notification of the June 2007 constructive discharge. The Plaintiff was also told she was not eligible for rehire because of the misdemeanor charge she mysteriously incurred after her constructive discharge. The Defendant XYZ Company was aware of the frivolous charge against Plaintiff for domestic dispute when she rehired with the Defendant but after Plaintiff's constructive discharge the domestic dispute charge resurrected itself.

Defendant XYZ Company employee John Doe had other complaints filed against him for similar conduct but XYZ did not take action to correct the problem (EXHIBIT 13 see Declaration of "Susan Doe Witness"). However, Defendant XYZ intentionally misstates in its Motion for Summary Judgment that John Doe with "twenty years of service had no prior discipline."

1. The terms of Jane Doe's employment regarding transfers are covered by Department Policy that exist between XYZ Company and the Union.

Defendant XYZ Company policy provides that an employee who is to be transferred to another location will receive a two-week notification. The Defendant has failed to show why Jane Doe did not receive such a notice. Upon Jane Doe notifying management that she had had enough, she was then told she was being reassigned to another office. Even though the XYZ Company policy requires a two-week notification prior to a transfer, it gave Plaintiff an improper notice directing her to move within a three-day period. Other XYZ Company employees who have been transferred have been given proper notice as required by policy.

Upon Jane Doe filing her complaint against John Doe, he was allowed to stay in the Western District office until Jane Doe further complained of John Doe's retaliation. Plaintiff filed against John Doe on December 19, 2006, and he was not removed until December 20, 2006, being placed on leave with pay. John Doe continued to call the Plaintiff even after he was removed (EXHIBIT 1). John Doe was a twenty-year XYZ Company veteran with a lot of department friends who were left in place to finish the retaliation of John Doe (his wife and Mr. Joe Doe). The Department allowed John Doe to come to the Plaintiff's office on several occasions to intimidate the Plaintiff. (EXHIBIT N, p. 32, EXHIBIT S2, p. 41 of Declaration of Jane Doe). However, Jane Doe was treated differently when she was disciplined on the same day she became aware of a complaint that was supposedly filed two months prior. After Ms. Jane Doe's complaint was known, she was retaliated against by others who were longtime friends of John Doe.

2. **Plaintiff's sex discrimination claim is not barred by any statute of limitation.**

Plaintiff Jane Doe presents facts that show discrete acts of single occurrences of harassment and retaliation that is connected to prior acts as background information to Plaintiffs sex discrimination complaint. On February 28, 2007, John Doe's wife entered into the Plaintiff's office area and harassed her, specifically for the purpose of letting the Plaintiff know she did not appreciate her ruining John Doe's career with Defendant XYZ Company. On June 7, 2007, based on XYZ Company's failure to comply with department policy, specifically for the purpose of preventing Plaintiff the opportunity to her due process rights, the Defendant reassigned the Plaintiff without notice or fair warning (EXHIBIT Y, p. 50-53). In *Burlington Northern & Santa Fe Railway Co. v. White*, 548 U.S. 53 (2006), the Court held that "the antiretaliation provision covers only those employer actions that would have been materially adverse to a reasonable employee." In support of the Plaintiff's claim, the Burlington Court in its holding stated "a reassignment of duties can constitute retaliatory discrimination where both the former and the present duties fall within the same job description." The Plaintiff's reassignment to another parole office with the same job description constitutes a materially adverse action under the Burlington decision.

An unlawful employment practice is a discrete act or single occurrence even when it has connections to other acts. *National Railroad Passenger Corporation v. Morgan*, 536 U.S. 101 111, 122 S. Ct. 2061 (2002). The Supreme Court has further stated that a timely charge of discrimination with the EEOC is not a jurisdictional prerequisite to a suit in federal court, but a requirement that, like a statute of limitations, is subject to waiver, estoppel, and equitable tolling. Id 113. The acts of defendants herein give rise to waiver and estoppel, and equitable tolling based on the failure to apply policy preventing harassment and retaliatory acts and continuing unfulfilled promises to the plaintiff that prevented her from constructively discharging on two different occasions.

However, even as a minimum, plaintiff Jane Doe has stated as least one incident within the appropriate statute of limitation that allows her to raise the other issues as background information to show a pattern and continuing course of illegal conduct by the defendants. The Plaintiff has shown through her affidavits, declaration, and pleadings that there was a hostile work environment, as well as specific acts of discrimination, that caused her constructive discharge. Hostile environment claims are different from discrete acts because their very nature involves repeated conduct (*National Railroad Passenger Corp v. Morgan*, Supra.536 U.S. at

115). It may occur over a series of days or perhaps years but has a direct contact to a discrete single act of harassment that may not be actionable on its own.

There are facts that XYZ Company employees made repeated comments to the Plaintiff, subjected the Plaintiff to work in high-risk locations without assistance, observed and harassed by management, frequent visits to her office, confronted by John Doe's spouse (office was gone through on several occasions, files rearranged, computer accessed and emails gone through, rumors were spread to other suites within the complex and Plaintiff was questioned.) (EXHIBIT N, p. 32, O, p. 33, W, p. 48, S-1, p. 40, S-2 p. 41 of Declaration of Jane Doe.) As per Title VII, the scope of the prohibition against discrimination is not limited to economic or tangible discrimination, and it covers more than terms and conditions of the employment in the narrow contract sense. Id 115-116.

There are disputed facts as far as the prior incidences being actionable, but as a minimum, there are actual claims within the required statute of limitations period.

3. Standards for Summary Judgment

To determine if a moving party for Summary Judgment has met its burden of proof, the District Court must view all evidence and inferences to be draw from it in a light most favorable to the party opposing the Motion. *Blackburne v. American Telephone and Telephone System*, 925 F. Supp. 762 (N.D.Ga. 1995). The Court is not to resolve conflicts among the evidence in dealing with Motions for Summary Judgment but is to review the evidence in the light most favorable to the non-moving party. *Matlock v. National Union Fire Ins, Cov.*, 925 F. Supp. 468 (E.D. Tex. 1996). When ruling on a Motion for Summary Judgment, the Court must construe the evidence in its most favorable light in favor of the party opposing the Motion and against the moving party. Further, the papers supporting the moving party are closely scrutinized, whereas the opponent's are indulgently treated. *Austin v. Bell*, 938 F. Supp. 1308 (M.S. Tenn. 1996).

Argument I
Defendant XYZ Company's affirmative defense claim was lost when the Defendant reassigned the Plaintiff.

The Supreme Court has held that an employer is liable for actionable hostile environment

sexual harassment by a supervisor with immediate (or higher) authority over the harassed employee. *Burlington Indus., Inc. v. Ellerth* 524 U.S. 724 (1998); *Faragher v. City of Boca Raton*, 524 U.S. 775. (1998). The Courts discussed in it posture if the supervisor's harassment culminates in . . . reassignment, the employer is liable and has no affirmative defense. The harasser must be the one who imposes the adverse action, unless there is evidence of a conspiracy between the decision maker and the harasser. *Murray v. Chi. Transit Auth.*, 252 F.3d 880 (7th Cir. 2001). Evidence will show, as discussed below, that the Plaintiff was subjected to an administrative transfer without her due processes adhered to by the Defendant, XYZ Company.

Therefore, we can only infer this material fact "in the light most favorable" to the nonmoving part that managers and/or supervisor conspired to retaliate against Plaintiff Jane Doe. According to the Defendant's policy, the Plaintiff would have been entitled to a two-week notice prior to being required to move from the location she was occupying. The same decision makers who removed the Plaintiff's perpetrator were the same ones who decided to remove the Plaintiff, which resulted in an adverse action.

Argument II

As a matter of law, the Defendant cannot assert a *Faragher/Ellerth* affirmative defense under the high Court's strict scrutiny test without proper application.

In a *Faragher* world, the Court applies the phase "looking to the reasonableness of the employer's conduct as well as that of the plaintiff victim," *Faragher*, 524 U.S. at 786-810, in order to require lower courts to test the weight of evidence by passing it through a screening analysis. In the same sense, the Court held in the same year in the *Ellerth* decision ". . . an employee who refuses the unwelcome and threatening sexual advances of a supervisor, yet suffers no adverse, tangible job consequences, may recover against the employer without showing the employer is negligent or otherwise at fault for the supervisor's actions," *Ellerth* 524 U.S. at 751-766.

The plain English language imposed by these Courts did not intend for lower courts to look solely at the amount of damages suffered by the plaintiff victim, but rather subject the parties ". . . to proof by a preponderance of the evidence" *Faragher*, 524 U.S. at 807, that requires "the Court assumes an important premise yet to be established . . ." *Ellerth* 524 U.S. 742 (Holding). The Plaintiff charges against the Department XYZ Company that it has used the constructions of the Courts to produce an absurd result against the *Kirby* decision, which stated plainly that "general terms should be so limited in their application as not to lead to injustice, oppression or absurd consequences." *United States v. Kirby* 74 U.S. (7 Wall) 482, 486 (1868). This principle applies with equal force to a statue written with clear language. XYZ Company attempts to hurdle a trial by jury by applying the "no tangible employment action" posture under the *Faragher/Ellerth* affirmative defense theory but fails to proportionately show how there is no tangible employment action which ". . . is designed to provide a framework for carefully examining the importance and the sincerity of the government's reasons for using no ("economic harm suffered") [race] in a particular context. *Grutter v. Bollinger et al* 539 at 326-327.

The Plaintiff's and Defendant's context matters when reviewing such action, *Gomillion v. Lightfoot*, 364 U. S. 339, 343-344, especially in a case where the Plaintiff has been constructively discharged. The agency's reason for terminating a twenty-year employee with no prior discipline is suspect and requires its context to be extracted. In fact, Jane Doe had a conversation with Ms. Angela Viva about John Doe sexual misconduct at the Southwest Parole office, which included references about sexual physical contract John Doe had with Sue Hancock, a department employee. Apparently, these incidents had been reported but covered up.

Argument III
Defendant has failed to show the essential elements in its use of *Faragher/Ellerth*.

The Celotex Court mentioned in its holding the phrase "element essential" on two different occasions. The word "element" in one instance is positioned later than the word "essential." This suggests the terms share equal force in their use by the Courts. The language essential element, as presented, shares it positions in the holding for similar existing purposes: to direct lower courts to ensure there is no genuine issue as to any material fact as it relates to a party's "showing sufficient to establish the existence of an element essential to that party's case" *Celotex Corp v. Catrett,* 477 U.S. 317 (1986). The Court of Appeals decision was reversed and remanded by the US Supreme Court because the Appeals Court's decision to reverse the lower court's decision on summary judgment was not supported by sufficient evidence.

Essentially, the message the Supreme Court sent was that even with pleadings, depositions, answers to interrogatories, there must not be an "essential element" in dispute by the nonmoving party. In whole, the Court paved the way for nonmoving party's to show the "existence of an essential element of its case with respect to which it has the burden of proof" Id at 322-323. In its lightest sense, a party without an essential element will naturally fail the burden of proof standard.

The plain language made it clear that the moving party is only "entitled to a judgment as a matter of law." *Celotex* 477 U.S. at 318 (if the nonmoving party failed to show the existence of an essential element.) The Courts did not make it clear whether it was referring to the prong elements in establishing the prima facie requirements.

If it did intend the word "element" to serve its purpose in that manner, it would have set the courts up to literally allow all discrimination cases though the door, which could establish the prima facie element. At the outset, a prima facie is not a hard test to prove. On the other hand, if the Court intended the bar to be set high by requiring a party to show that an essential element is proving an occurrence, then an essential element is a genuine issue of material fact and would tend to negate a moving party's position in seeking a summary judgment.

Argument IV
The Department misapplies the law of materiality in determining liable for the sexual misconduct of John Doe.

The violation of department policy regarding sexual harassment is a violation which is material and becomes a matter of fact when it occurs because of the violation of written policy. The common-law doctrine of respondent superior was established to define the legal liability of an employer for the actions of an employee.

The doctrine was adopted in the United States and has been a fixture of agency law. It provides a better chance for an injured party to actually recover damages, because under respondent superior, the employer is liable for the injuries caused by an employee who is working within the scope of his employment relationship. It is clear that the actions taken by the department in suspending John Doe and then terminating his employment meets the standard test of being egregious enough to meet the Courts test as it applies to meeting the severe and pervasive standard. We have to ask why a twenty-year XYZ Company veteran with no other infractions would be terminated. This alone is suspect.

Absent the remedial actions taken by the Department in suspending John Doe and later terminating his employment, it is plausible/probable there is a cover up of his propensity to engage in aggressive behavior, violence, lying, or other forms of moral turpitude. Without further inquiry, it would skirt the potential to locate witnesses to testify to those traits. The record as it stands shows that John Doe had subjected the Department to at least one other EEOC investigation because of sexual misconduct.

Regardless of the XYZ Company's actions, the harm has already been done and was not taken back when John Doe was removed. Jane Doe suffered sleep disturbances, dramatic weight fluctuations, changes in her eating patterns, unexplained physical symptoms, low self-esteem, and social phobia and developed a distrust of men as a result of John Doe's sexual bullying.

On several occasions, Jane Doe was told by her family to seek counseling, but she refused because she could not afford the cost. Despite XYZ Company's remedial actions against John Doe, the touching of Jane Doe is a material harm in which she suffered and cannot be taken back through the XYZ's remedial actions. At no time has XYZ's defense stated that Jane Doe was not touched by John Doe in the manner in which she claims. In fact, Jane Doe has several reliable witnesses. The only opposition to the materiality of the sexual harassment XYZ makes is to the exchanged one-time period of emails Jane Doe had with John Doe in which they use to suggest Jane Doe's willingness to participate. XYZ fails to show how the material touching affected Jane Doe, though.

The material facts are the most important ones that decide the outcome of the case. When the touching of Jane Doe became unwanted and/or unwarranted, she established a material claim. Keep in mind that they never started out as wanted. It is irrelevant whether the touching was harmful. Department policy does not discuss sexual harassment being harmful, but it does imply or express it being offensive. That is what employment law sexual harassment is all about: preventing offensive behavior.

Let's consider that Jane Doe and John Doe had a sexual relationship, and one of them said no to sexual intercourse just before a hot discussion of sex and one continued to force intercourse on the unwanted. That person would be liable for assault and battery. Jane Doe was in apprehension to a battery because of the intentional acts of John Doe's of unwanted touching. Had Jane Doe been kicked in the face and knocked unconscious, no one would question if it were harmful. Regardless, the kicking would not be an issue as a matter of fact and would only have force as a matter of the law if a statute stated it is illegal to make even a professional boxer apprehensive to the touching.

Violating a written established policy, law, or regulation in itself is considered a genuine issue of material of fact. Thus, John Doe, who is a twenty-year department veteran, had an existing duty to meet the standard of care in accordance to existing Department policy on sexual harassment.

If a police officer stops a driver and beats the driver unconscious and the Department terminates the officer several months later, it is still liable for the injuries caused of its agents and must pay damages to the victimized driver. The Department cannot escape liability because it fired the police officer. Similarly, neither can XYZ Company escape liability on the basis it suspended and fired Jane Doe's perpetrator. Jane Doe has sufficiently shown that she was subjected to a transfer and has provided the employer's statement as proof or lack thereof that she was transferred without her due process rights intact. Therefore, she has met the essential element of her case with respect to which she has the burden of proof.

Argument V
The Defense of having an effective procedure for handling complaints is not available when the liability of discrimination is created by acts of employees.

The Courts have held ". . . where the plaintiff did not suffer any 'tangible' employment action such as [constructive] discharge or demotion, but rather suffered 'intangible' harm flowing from harassment that is sufficiently severe or pervasive to create a hostile work environment" *Faragher v. City of Boca*, 524 U.S. 775, 808 (1998). It is sufficient enough to warrant a jury instruction. In *Faragher and Burlington Indus., Inc. v. Ellerth*, 524 U.S. U.S. 742, the Courts held an employer is strictly liable for supervisor harassment that "culminates in a tangible employment action, such as discharge . . . or undesirable reassignment". *Ellerth*, 524 U.S. U.S. at 765.

The Plaintiff has shown to the Court's requirement, at minimum, that she was subjected to an administrative transfer to another region without her due process rights entitlement to a two-week notification or other remedies. The reassignment occurred because of a false complaint filed by a coworker(s), which gives rise to the validity of Defendants Affirmative defense. The Respondent has failed to show reasons for this administrative transfer. When such action is taken, the *Faragher/Ellerth* courts have regarded the guideline of an affirmative defense to liability to be void. The Department has failed to meet this test.

Besides the affirmative defense provided by *Ellerth*, the absence of a tangible employment action also justifies requiring the Plaintiff to prove a further element in order to protect the employer from unwarranted liability for the discriminatory acts of its nonsupervisor employees. However, respondent superior liability for the acts of nonsupervisory employees exist only where "the defendant knew or should have known of the harassment and failed to take prompt remedial action." *Andrews v. City of Philadelphia*, 895 F.2d 1469, 1486 (3rd Cir. 1990).

Jane Doe's constructive discharge is attached to the genesis of her sexual harassment complaint, and the deterrence element of employer liability for the acts of nonsupervisory employees still exist in which the Department has not confronted. In *Pennsylvania State Police v. Suders*, 542 U.S. 129, 138-141 (2004), the Court considered the relationship between constructive discharge brought by supervisor harassment and the affirmative defense articulated in *Ellerth/Faragher*.

The question lingers in Jane Doe's case whether XYZ charged John Doe with harassment or let him escape a charge of harassment by forwarding him the outcome of the investigation allowing him to resign without penalty. The Court concluded in *Ellerth/Faragher* that "absent such a "tangible employment action," the defense is available to the employer who supervisors are charged with harassment. The question of whether a particular act is retaliatory is a question of law; whether the activity is retaliatory is a question of fact for the jury. Not to allow a trial by jury in this matter would shock the conscience of our society and offend the judicial notion of fairness.

Argument VI
Defendant's stated reason for the Administrative Transfer is pretextual and violates Sections 703(a)(1).

In *McDonald Douglas Corp. v. Green*, 411 U.S. 792, the Court produced the standard of proof to determine pretext when looking to the defendant's use of general policy. On that note, the Green Court reasoned that "statistics as to petitioner's employment policy and practice may be helpful to a determination of whether petitioner's refusal to rehire respondent in this case conformed to a general pattern of discrimination against blacks." *Jones v. Lee Way Motor Freight, Inc.*, 431 F.2d 245 (CA10 1970); Blumrosen, Strangers in Paradise: *Griggs v. Duke Power Co.* and the Concept of Employment Discrimination, 71 Mich.L.Rev. 59, 91-94 (1972).

On or about Thursday, June 7, 2007, Jane Doe notified the Department of her constructive discharge. Mysteriously, on the day of her discharge notice, management notified Jane Doe she was being transferred to the Northern District Office that would require her to report by June 11, 2007. Department policy dictates an employee is to be given a two-week advance notice prior to a transfer.

The record is not clear on the requirements for an administrative transfer. However, the record does not indicate that Jane Doe was entitled to her due process of being notified of an alleged reason for the transfer. To illustrate, after Jane Doe announced her constructive discharge, she was told she was under investigation regarding a complaint about her conduct which was allegedly lodged against her two months prior of her discharge date. However, Jane Doe knew absolutely nothing about the alleged complaint. Therefore, she had been deprived of notice and fair warning and the ability to have an administrative hearing on the charges against her.

Thus, Jane Doe contends the transfer is a pretext for a cover up, which is against Department policy, and the facts surrounding the matter must be drawn out to test its context.

Argument VII
Defendant may not rely on an Affirmative Defense in a Motion for Summary Judgment where there is a genuine issue as to any material fact.

As stated infra, the affirmative defense is misapplied in dictum. As charged, the Defendant has failed to refer to any "pleadings, depositions, answers to interrogatories, and admissions on file, together with the affidavits" *Celotex Corp. v. Catrett,* 477 U.S. 317 (1986).

At best, the defendant has relied on self-assessments as provided in their Motion which is full of absurd references that will require a tier-of-fact to decipher. Under *Adickes v. S.H. Kress & Co.,* 398 U.S. 144 1970, the Court set a strong foundation for a nonmoving party to survive a summary judgment motion where the moving party has "failed to allege any facts from which a conspiracy might be inferred." On the basis of the record, the Agency has blatantly failed to show the involvement of Plaintiff's coworkers and new supervisors during and after the date of John Doe's six-month paid period of leave.

The *Adickes* Court reversed the summary judgment against the nonmoving party because "the District Court erred in granting summary judgment on the conspiracy count." *Adickes* 398 U.S. at 149-161. The *Adickes* Court further charged that "Respondent did not carry out its burden, as the party moving for summary judgment of showing the absence of a genuine issue as to any material fact as it did not foreclose [*emphasis added*] the possibility that there was a policeman in the store while the petitioner was awaiting service (from which the jury could infer an understanding between the officer and an employee of respondent that petitioner not be served), and its failure to meet that burden requires reversal." 398 U. S. at 153-159.

The Agency's Motion for Summary Judgment has failed to foreclose genuine issues of material facts regarding the immediate after math of John Doe's removal. The Plaintiff has met the burden showing that she had received phone calls from John Doe at her place of employment in which he attempted to persuade Plaintiff "to drop the issues." This continued harassment makes John Does removal void because he continued to make contact with Plaintiff. As charged by Plaintiff in accordance to rule Fed.

Rule Civ. Proc. 56(e), she is "not required to come forward with suitable opposing affidavits." In this instance matter, however, the Plaintiff has come forth with a pile of evidence supporting her claim of retaliation as it relates to her sexual harassment claim.

Argument VIII
The Defendant has intentionally misapplied the *Faragher v. City of Boca*, 524 U.S. 775 in dictum.

The *Faragher* Court held "An employer is vicariously liable for actionable discrimination caused by a supervisor, but subject to an affirmative defense looking to the reasonableness of the employer's conduct as well as that of the plaintiff victim".

The Department relies on prong B of the *Faragher* test but fails to proffer its ". . . proven mechanism for reporting and resolving sexual complaints of sexual harassment, available to the employee with undue risk or expense." *Faragher v. City of Boca*, 524 U.S. at 806. In *Cerros v. Steel Technologies, Inc.* 398 F.3d 944 (7th Cir. 2004), the Court stated that the Plaintiff need not follow the letter of the employer's harassment reporting procedure if the employer had notice of the harassment. In this instant matter, the Plaintiff's go-to person was her harasser, thus leaving the Plaintiff temporarily stunned. But this was not the only harassment by John Doe—this was a steady stream, and the *Loughman* Court said that "The existence of a steady stream of harassment is the evidence that the employer's harassment policy is not effective. *Loughman v. Malnati Org.*, 395 F. ed 404 (7th Cir.2005). In support of the Plaintiff, an affirmative defense is not available when the employer fails to name a person to whom an employee may complain. *Gentry v. Exp. Packaging Co.*, 238 F. 3d 842 (7th Cir. 2001). Defendant XYZ Company policy is not posted but rather an annual training and is not regularly updated to affect the law under the Gentry decision. Therefore, the Plaintiff did not know whom she needed to complain regarding the harassment, thus making the Defendant's sexual harassment policy ineffective. The record shows that others who were subjected to sexual harassment were retaliated against. This is more than an unresolved issue suggesting complainers have to fear reporting Title VII violations. More likely, it is the ground where this claim stands on. In fact, the Department shows a willingness to wrap up this complaint, which would limit testimony on other investigations in which John Doe may or should have been subject to.

To illustrate, Sue Hancock, a former XYZ employee, filed charges with the EEOC for John Doe's sexual misconduct. However, Defendant Counsel has stated in the Motion for Summary Judgment that John Doe has worked for XYZ Company for more than twenty years with no prior discipline. Evidence shows John Doe was moved to the Western district under an administrative transfer for alleged sexual misconduct. This is a genuine issue of material fact in dispute and as a matter of law "... disputes over facts that might affect the outcome of the suit . . . will properly preclude the entry of summary judgment" *Anderson v. Liberty Lobby, Inc.* 477 U.S. 242, 248 (1986).

Argument IX
The Agency erroneously applies *Faragher v. City of Boca*, 524 U.S. 775 and *Burlington Indus., Inc. v. Ellerth*, 524 U.S. U.S. 742 in asserting an affirmative defense on Plaintiff's lack of damages and failure to report.

The Defendant relies, in part, on *King v. AC & R Advertising*, 65 F.3d 764 F.3d 764, 767 (9th Cir. 1995) to gain summary judgment but mistakenly has supported the Plaintiff's claim of constructive discharge which is open to an entitlement of a trial by jury to "show that the conditions giving rise to [her] his resignation [are] were extraordinary and egregious". Id at 767-68. Defense counsel has misapplied the standard in which Plaintiff's constructive discharge has risen.

In *Poland v. Chertoff,* 494 F.3d 1174, 1184 (9th Cir. 2007), the Court stated that the bar was set high for an action of a claim for constructive discharge "because federal antidiscrimination policies are better served when the employee and employer attack discrimination within their existing employment relationship, rather than when the employee walks away and then litigates whether his employment situation was intolerable." The question presents itself, "Did Plaintiff in this matter walk away?" Not likely so. In fact, the work atmosphere was so hostile that Jane Doe attempted to constructively discharge on two other occasions, but she was discouraged by management with what would be discovered later by Jane Doe as empty promises.

Again, there is a genuine issue of material fact in dispute. After Plaintiff's complaint was exposed to other staff, she was subjected to retaliation by John Doe's wife and coworkers; forced to work in an area normally staffed by two parole officers (against department past policy); disciplined for objecting to a reassignment; constant surveillance of her computer files (keep in mind the agency failed to observe her supervisor's emails); and was ridiculed, shunned, embarrassed, harassed, and given unjustified performance evaluations after her complaints.

However, the Defense counsel would make it appear that Plaintiff filed a complaint on day one and quit on day two. Anyone would find this scenario unreasonable, however.

Argument X
A Moving Party may not rely on lack of damages to survive a motion for summary judgment.

As Plaintiff has already charged that "The court must consider all materials in the light most favorable to the party opposing the motion for summary judgment." See *Adickes v. S.H. Kress & Co.,* 398 U.S. 144, (1970), and *Celotex Corp. v. Catrett,* 477 U.S. 317 (1986).

These plain-English decisions make it clear that the post decision to *Adickes* and *Celotex* as applied later under *Faragher v. City of Boca*, 524 U.S. 775 and *Burlington Indus., Inc. v. Ellerth*, 524 U.S. U.S. 742 require the Courts to apply the Affirmative Defense standard of ". . . looking to the reasonableness of the employer's conduct as well as that of the plaintiff victim" *Faragher* 524 U.S. 786-810. When this standard is applied, a question of damages does not arise until the moment of truth: before a jury.

As a matter of law, the Plaintiff is entitled to consideration of emotional distress damages, which do not require medical evidence. *Farfaras v. Citizens Bank*, 433 F. 3d 558 (7th Cir. 2006.); Section 701 et seq., 42 U.S.C.A Sect. 200 ect. Seq. The record shows that Jane Doe has provided the names of at least two witnesses who can testify to the "emotional distress" suffered by her resulting from the defendants conduct.

The Plaintiff has presented names of witnesses who may provide testimony to her emotional distress claim as well as to all claims submitted by her complaint. Moreover, section 706(g) of Title VII states that back pay can be recovered for up to two years prior to filing a charge with the EEOC, a period that reaches back more than a year before the start of the 180/300-day filing period. A continuing violation theory applies where the protected activity previously asserted is the ". . . product of an intent to discriminate" *Lorance v. AT&T Technologies* 490 U.S. 900. In this case, Jane Doe's perpetrator was two days after the Department became aware of the sexual harassment. The Department acted to terminate John Doe only upon the receipt of an EEOC notification.

It may appear at first blush that the agency played its cards by not affecting John Doe's career by keeping his career intact while conspiring to change (time bar) the outcome of the Plaintiff's ability to file in a timely manner on the issues of sexual harassment. Regardless of the Department's argument, the *Teamsters* Court would allow the Plaintiff to argues that the constructive discharge "had its genesis in the [sex] discrimination," *Teamsters v. United States*, 431 U.S. 324, 356, which provides Jane Doe with enough clay to mold the statues in question to a claim against the Department. To emphasize, the Agency's reason for terminating a twenty-year employee with no prior discipline is suspect and requires its context to be revealed.

A person previously accused of sexual harassment should not have been in position to establish another Title VII action. The employer's stated reason of applying the affirmative defense under Faragher/Ellerth, as applied by the department, are void for its vagueness.

Conclusion

For the above-stated reasons, for the Motion for Summary should be denied.

Dated this 4th day of February 2010.

_____

Jane Doe, Pro Per

Appendix I

Guerilla Tactics Checklist

- Find the occupational series in your job field at www.usajobs.gov. Remember that you can find the complete list all occupational series on the second page of this site.
- Cut and paste the occupational series of your choice. Be sure to include its number. Google it.
- Once you Google and locate the PDF of the occupational series, develop a resume for each occupational series. You should have at least five resumes. (When you Google your occupational series, you will find several links that will take you directly to the Office of Personnel Management site. This is not what you're looking for. Locate the PDF of the occupational series in your field. I cannot stress this enough. Once you find OPM's language of your occupational series, your resume will be improved and get you past the language and code words of OPM's requirements).
- Create a file and save all your applications, certificates, military transcripts, college transcripts, resumes, SF-15, DD-124, etc.
- Submit a cover letter that makes it clear you want to be considered under the Veterans VRA and VEOA.
- Submit OF-306. (This form will clear up any doubts of determining whether you are suitable for federal employment.)
- Once you have submitted your application and you believe your preference rights were violated, you must file a complaint with the Department of Labor within 60 days of when you become away of the violation.

- Once the Department of Labor has made a decision on your alleged preference rights violation, prepare to file your appeal with the Merit System Protection Board within the required time limitation period. Do not allow the Department of Labor's decision sway your decision to file an appeal with the MSPB.

APPENDIX J

DIRECTORY FOR VEOA REGIONAL AND STATE OFFICES

Boston	Connecticut	Maine
Boston Veterans' Employment and Training Service, U.S. Department of Labor J.F. Kennedy Federal Building, Room E-315 Boston, Massachusetts 02203 Phone: (617) 565-2080 Fax: (617) 565-2082	**Connecticut** Veterans' Employment and Training Service U.S. Department of Labor 200 Folly Brook Boulevard Wethersfield, Connecticut 06109 Phone: (860) 263-6490 Fax: (860) 263-6498	**Maine** Veterans' Employment and Training Service U.S. Department of Labor 5 Mollison Way Suite 104 Lewiston, Maine 04240 Phone: (207) 753-9089 Fax: (207) 783-5304
Massachusetts Veterans' Employment and Training Service U.S. Department of Labor C.F. Hurley Building 19 Staniford Street, 1st Floor Boston, Massachusetts 02114 Phone: (617) 626-6699 Fax: (617) 727-2330	**New Hampshire** Veterans' Employment and Training Service U.S. Department of Labor James C. Cleveland Federal Bldg., Room #3602 53 Pleasant Street Concord, New Hampshire 03301 Phone: (603) 225-1424 Fax: (603) 225-1545	**New Jersey** U.S. Department of Labor Veterans' Employment and Training Service 1 John Fitch Plaza Labor Building, 10th Floor P.O. Box 058 Trenton, New Jersey 08625 Phone: (609) 292-2930 Fax: (609) 292-9070
New York U.S. Department of Labor Veterans' Employment and Training Service Harriman State Campus Bldg. 12, Room 518 Albany, New York 12240-0099 Phone: (518) 457-7465 Fax: (518) 435-0833	**New York** Clark Hall Rm. B-1-40 10720 Mt. Belvedere Blvd. Ft. Drum, NY 13602 Phone: (315) 772-0837 Fax: (315) 772-7720	**New York** Veterans' Employment and Training Service U.S. Department of Labor 9 Bond Street, Rm. 302 Brooklyn, NY 11201 Phone: (718) 613-3676 Fax: (718) 613-3685

Puerto Rico and Virgin Islands	Rhode Island	Vermont
U.S. Department of Labor Veterans' Employment and Training Service Roberto H. Todd Avenue 501 Parada 18 Santurce, Puerto Rico 00907-3905 Phone: (787) 754-5391 Fax: (787) 754-2983	U.S. Department of Labor Veterans' Employment and Training Service Dr. John E. Donley Rehabilitation Center Rhode Island Department of Labor and Training 249 Blackstone Blvd. Providence, RI 02906 Phone: (401) 243-1281 Fax: (401) 243-1240	Veterans' Employment and Training Service U.S. Department of Labor 81 River Street, Suite 207 Montpelier, Vermont 05602 Phone: (802) 828-2057 Fax: (802) 828-2069
Philadelphia Region	**Philadelphia Region**	**Philadelphia Region**
Veterans' Employment and Training Service U.S. Department of Labor The Curtis Center VETS/770 West 170 S. Independence Mall West Philadelphia, Pennsylvania 19106-3310 Phone: (304) 528-5873 Fax: (304) 528-5874	U.S. Department of Labor Veterans' Employment and Training Service 2699 Park Avenue, Suite 240, Room A04 Huntington, WV 25704 Phone: (304) 558-4001 Fax: (304) 344-4591	U.S. Department of Labor Veterans' Employment and Training Service Capitol Complex, Room 112F 112 California Avenue Charleston, West Virginia 25305-0112 Phone: (304) 558-4001 Fax: (304) 344-4591
Delaware	**District of Columbia**	**Maryland**
U.S. Department of Labor Veterans' Employment and Training Service 4425 North Market Street, Annex Room 108 Wilmington, Delaware 19802-0828 Phone: (302) 761-8138/9 Fax: (302) 761-4676	U.S. Department of Labor 4058 Minnesota Avenue, N.E. Suite 4007 Washington, DC 20019-3540 Phone: (202) 671-2179 Fax: (202) 671-1503	Phone: (410) 767-2110/2111 Fax: (410) 333-5136 U.S. Department of Labor Veterans' Employment and Training Service 1100 North Eutaw Street, Room 201 Baltimore, Maryland 21201
Maryland	**Pennsylvania**	**Pennsylvania**
Phone: (301) 393-8253 Fax: (301) 393-2654 U.S. Department of Labor Veterans' Employment and Training Service 14 N. Potomac St. Suite 100 Hagerstown, Maryland 21740	Phone: (717) 787-5834, 5835 Fax: (717) 783-2631 U.S. Department of Labor Veterans' Employment and Training Service Labor and Industry Bldg., Room 1106 651 Boas St Harrisburg, Pennsylvania 17121	Phone: (814) 445-4161 x239 Fax: (814) 445-3913 U.S. Department of Labor Veterans' Employment and Training Service Somerset Job 218 North Kimberly Avenue Somerset, PA 15501-4161

Pennsylvania Phone: (412) 552-7023 Fax: (412) 552-7051 U.S. Department of Labor Veterans' Employment and Training Service Pittsburgh Downtown Career Link, 22nd Floor 425 6th Avenue Pittsburgh, Pennsylvania 15219	**Pennsylvania** Phone: (717) 783-8113 Fax: (717) 783-2631 U.S. Department of Labor Veterans' Employment and Training Service Labor and Industry Bldg., Room 1106 651 Boas St Harrisburg, Pennsylvania 17121	**Pennsylvania** Phone: (717) 787-5834 Fax: (717) 783-2631 U.S. Department of Labor Veterans' Employment and Training Service Labor and Industry Bldg., Room 1106 651 Boas St Harrisburg, Pennsylvania 17121
Virginia Phone: (804) 786-7270, 7269, 5436 Fax: (804) 786-4548 U.S. Department of Labor Veterans' Employment and Training Service 707 East Main Street, Room 350 Richmond, Virginia 23219	**West Virginia** Phone: (304) 558-4001 Fax: (304) 344-4591 U.S. Department of Labor Veterans' Employment and Training Service Capitol Complex, Room 112F 112 California Avenue Charleston, West Virginia 25305-0112	**Atlanta Region** Veterans' Employment and Training Service U.S. Department of Labor Sam Nunn Atlanta Federal 61 Forsyth Street, S.W., Room 6T85 Atlanta, Georgia 30303 Phone: (404) 562-2305-2310
Alabama U.S. Department of Labor 649 Monroe Street, Room 2218 Montgomery, AL 36131-0001 FTS: (334) 223-7677 Fax: (334) 242-8927 Modem #: (334) 240-3056 COMM: (334) 242-8115 (Also serves as answering machine)	**Florida** Phone: (904) 353-2187 Fax: (904) 359-6151 Veterans' Employment and Training Service U.S. Department of Labor 215 Market Street, Suite 300 Jacksonville, Florida 32202-2851	**Florida** Phone: (954) 677-5818 Fax: (954) 677-5816 Veterans' Employment and Training Service U.S. Department of Labor 2550 West Oakland Park Boulevard—Room 133 Ft. Lauderdale, Fl. 33311 FTS: (727) 324-2847 Fax: (727) 324-2855 (coversheet required)
Florida Veterans' Employment and Training Service U.S. Department of Labor c/o Worknet Pinellas 38500 U.S. Highway 19 North North Palm Harbor, FL 34684 Phone: (727) 608-2495 Fax: (727) 328-3392 (coversheet required)	**Florida** Veterans' Employment and Training Service U.S. Department of Labor c/o Worknet Pinellas Shipping address: P.O. Box 56105 St. Petersburg, FL 33732 Physical address: 3420 8th Avenue South St. Petersburg, FL 33711	**Florida** U.S. Department of Labor Veterans' Employment and Training Service Tampa Bay Workforce Alliance 9215 N. Florida Ave STE 101 Tampa, FL 33612-7985 Phone: (813) 375-3999 Fax: (813) 375-3998

Georgia	Georgia	Kentucky
Phone: (404) 232-3870 FTS: (404) 331-3893 Fax: (404) 232-3874 Modem: #: (404) 656-9232 Veterans' Employment and Training Service U.S. Department of Labor 148 Andrew Young International Blvd. Suite 225 Atlanta, Georgia 30303-1732	Phone: (706) 5458408 Phone: (706) 545-8295 SRP Building #2784 Sightseeing Road at Dixie Road Ft. Benning, GA 31905-3525 COMM (706) 545-8408	Phone: (502) 564-7062 Fax: (502) 564-1476 Modem #: (502) 564-2497 Veterans' Employment and Training Service U.S. Department of Labor Department for Employment Services 275 East Main Street 2nd Floor West—2WD Frankfort, Kentucky 40621-2339
Mississippi	**North Carolina**	**South Carolina**
Phone: (601) 321-6078 (Benjamin McCaffery) Phone: (601) 321-6235 (Robert Smith) Fax: (601) 321-6187 U.S. DOL/VETS 1235 Echelon Parkway Jackson, Mississippi 39215-1699	COMM: (919) 707-1944 FTS: (919) 856-4792 Modem #: (919) 733-0549 Fax: (919) 733-1508 Veterans' Employment and Training Service U.S. Department of Labor P.O. Box 27625 Raleigh, North Carolina 27611-7625 **Located at:** 700 Wade Avenue, Room G-217 Raleigh, North Carolina 27605-1154	COMM: (803)737- 7650; (803)737-7652; (803)737-7649 Fax: (803) 737-7656 FTS: (803)765-5195 Modem #: (803) 253-7651 Veterans' Employment and Training Service U.S. Department of Labor P.O. Box 1755 Columbia, South Carolina 29202-1755 **Located at:** Lem Harper Building 631 Hampton Street, Suite 141 Columbia, South Carolina 29201
Tennessee	**Tennessee**	**Chicago**
Phone: (931) 572-1688 Fax: (931) 648-6331 Veterans' Employment and Training Service U.S. Department of Labor 350 Pageant Lane STE 406 Clarksville, TN 37040 Phone: (931) 572-1688 Fax: (931) 648-6331	COMM: (615) 736-7680 or 5037 Fax: (615) 741-4241 Veterans' Employment and Training Service U.S. Department of Labor 2242 Rosa L. Parks Boulevard Nashville, TN 37228	Veterans' Employment and Training Service U.S. Department of Labor 230 South Dearborn, Room 1064 Chicago, Illinois 60604 Main Office (312) 353-0970

Illinois	Indiana	Iowa
Veterans' Employment and Training Service U.S. Department of Labor 33 South State Street, 8th Floor Room 8174 Chicago, Illinois 60603 Main Office (312) 793-3433 Fax: (312) 793-4795	Veterans' Employment and Training Service U.S. Department of Labor 10 North Senate Ave., Room SE 103 Indianapolis, Indiana 46204 Main Office (317) 232-6805 Fax (317) 233-5720	Veterans' Employment and Training Service U.S. Department of Labor 1000 E. Grand Avenue—1st Floor West Des Moines, Iowa 50319 Main Office (515) 281-9061 Fax (515) 281-9063
Kansas Phone: (785) 783-7070 Veterans' Employment and Training Service U.S. Department of Labor 900 S. Kansas Avenue, Suite 305 Topeka, Kansas 66612-1220 Main Office (785) 783-8263 Fax (785) 783-8542	**Michigan** Veterans' Employment and Training Service U.S. Department of Labor Victor Office Center, Suite 120 201 N. Washington Square Lansing, MI 48933 Main Office (517) 373-7094 Fax: (517) 373-1117	**Minnesota** Veterans' Employment and Training Service U.S. Department of Labor 332 Minnesota St., Suite W1372 St. Paul, MN 55101 Main Office (651) 259-7511/7512 Fax: (651) 282-2711
Missouri Veterans' Employment and Training Service U.S. Department of Labor 421 East Dunklin Street Jefferson City, MO 65101 Mailing Address: Veterans' Employment and Training Service U.S. Department of Labor P.O. Box 59 Jefferson City, MO 65101 Fax (573) 751-6710	**Nebraska** Veterans' Employment and Training Service U.S. Department of Labor c/o Nebraska Department of Labor 550 South 16th Street, Room 206 Lincoln, NE 68508 Mailing address: Veterans' Employment and Training Service U.S. Department of Labor c/o Nebraska Department of Labor P.O. Box 94600 Lincoln, NE 68509 Main Office (402) 471-9833 Fax (402) 471-2092	**Ohio** Veterans' Employment and Training Service U.S. Department of Labor 4020 East 5th Avenue, Room M-153 PO Box 1618 Columbus, Ohio 43219 Main Office (614) 466-2768 Fax (614) 752-5007

Wisconsin U.S. Department of Labor Veterans' Employment and Training Service 201 East Washington, GEF-1 Building, Room G109 Madison, WI 53703 Main Office (608) 266-3110 Fax (608) 261-6710	**Dallas Region** Phone: (972) 850-4715 Fax: (972) 850-4716 Veterans' Employment and Training Service U.S. Department of Labor 525 S. Griffin Street, Room 858 Dallas, TX 75202	**Dallas Region** Phone: (225) 389-0440 Fax: (225) 342-3152 Veterans' Employment and Training Service U.S. Department of Labor Louisiana Department of Labor Administration Building, Rm 184 1001 North 23rd Street Baton Rouge, Louisiana 70802 **Mailing address:** P.O. Box 94094, Room 184 Baton Rouge, Louisiana 70804-9094
Dallas Region Phone: (720) 264-3184 Fax: (720) 264-3197 Veterans' Employment and Training Service U.S. Dept. of Labor One Denver Federal Center Building 53, Room B1414 Lakewood, CO 80225 **Mailing address:** P.O. Box 25607 Lakewood, CO 80225-0607	**Arkansas** Phone: (501) 682-3786 Fax: (501) 682-3752 Veterans' Employment and Training Service U.S. Department of Labor Arkansas Department of Workforce Services Room 237, #2 Capitol Mall Little Rock, Arkansas 72201 **Mailing address:** P.O. Box 128	**Colorado** Veterans' Employment and Training Service U.S. Department of Labor 633 17th Street, Suite 700 Denver, Colorado 80202 Phone: (303) 318-8827 Fax: (303) 844-2017
Colorado Phone: (719) 226-8031 Fax: (719) 226-8032 Veterans' Employment and Training Service U.S. Department of Labor 2864 S. Circle Dr. Suite 375 Colorado Springs, CO 80906	**Louisiana** Phone: (225) 389-0339 Fax: (225) 342-3152 Veterans' Employment and Training Service U.S. Department of Labor Louisiana Department of Labor Administration Building, Room 184 1001 North 23rd Street Baton Rouge, Louisiana 70802 **Mailing address:** P.O. Box 94094, Room 184 Baton Rouge, LA 70804-9094	**Montana** Phone: (406) 447-3233/3239 Fax: (406) 447-3213 Veterans' Employment and Training Service U.S. Department of Labor P.O. Box 1728 Helena, Montana 59624-1728 **Located at:** 715 Front Street Helena, Montana 59601

New Mexico Phone: (505) 346-7502, 7503 Fax: (505) 242-6179 Veterans' Employment and Training Service U.S. Department of Labor 401 Broadway Blvd. NE Albuquerque, NM 87102-2301 **Mailing address:** P.O. Box 25085 Albuquerque, NM 87125-5085	**North Dakota** Phone: (701) 250-4337 Fax: (701) 328-2890 Veterans' Employment and Training Service U.S. Department of Labor 1000 E. Divide Avenue Bismarck, North Dakota 58501	**Oklahoma** Phone: (405) 231-5088 Phone: (405) 557-7189 Fax: (405) 557-7123 Veterans' Employment and Training Service U.S. Department of Labor 2401 N Lincoln Blvd, Room 304-2 Oklahoma City, Oklahoma 73105 **Mailing address:** P.O. Box 52003 Oklahoma City, OK 73152-2003
South Dakota Phone: (605) 626-2325 Fax: (605) 626-2359 **Mailing address:** Veterans' Employment and Training Service Department of Labor P.O. Box 4730 Aberdeen, SD 57402-4730 **Located at:** 420 South Roosevelt Street Aberdeen, South Dakota 57401-5131	**Texas** Phone: (512) 463-2816 Veterans' Employment and Training Service U.S. Department of Labor TWC Building, Room 516-T 1117 Trinity Street Austin, TX 78701 **Mailing address:** P.O. Box 1468 Austin, TX 78767	**Texas** Phone: (210) 582-1622 Fax: (210) 826-6068 Veterans' Employment and Training Service U.S. Department of Labor Workforce Solutions Alamo—Walzem 4615 Walzem Road, Suite 100 San Antonio, TX 78218-1610
Texas Phone: (915) 887-2624 Fax: (915) 629-2092 Veterans' Employment and Training Service U.S. Department of Labor 9740 Dyer Suite 110 El Paso, TX 79924	**Texas** Phone: (817) 336-3727 Ext. 1101 Fax: (817) 335-0731 Veterans' Employment and Training Service U.S. Department of Labor 301 W. 13th Street, Suite 407 Fort Worth, TX 76102-4699 **Mailing address:** P.O. Box 591 Fort Worth, TX 76101-0591	**Utah** Phone: (801) 524-5703 Fax: (801) 524-3099 Veterans' Employment and Training Service U.S. Department of Labor 140 East 300 South, Suite 209 Salt Lake City, UT 84111-2333

Wyoming	San Francisco Region	Alaska
Phone: (307) 261-5454 Phone: (307) 235-3281/3282 Fax: (307) 235-3272 **Mailing address:** Veterans' Employment and Training Service U.S. Department of Labor P.O. Box 2760 Casper, WY 82602-2760 **Located at:** 100 West Midwest Avenue Casper, WY 82601-2429	(Alaska, Arizona, California, Guam, Hawaii, Idaho, Nevada, Oregon and Washington) Phone: (415) 625-7675 Fax: (415) 625-7677 VPS-**Vacant** Veterans' Employment and Training Service U.S. Department of Labor 90 7th St. Suite 2-600	Phone: (907) 465-2723 Fax: (907) 465-5528 Veterans' Employment and Training Service U.S. Department of Labor P.O. Box 25509 Juneau, AK 99811-5509 Location: 1111 West 8th Street, Suite 306 Juneau, Alaska 99811-5509
Arizona Phone: (602) 542-2516 Fax: (602) 542-4103 Veterans' Employment and Training Service U.S. Department of Labor P.O. Box 6123-SC760E Phoenix, AZ 85005 Location: 1400 West Washington Street, Suite 123 Phoenix, AZ 85007	**California** Phone: (916) 654-8178 Fax: (916) 654-9469 Veterans' Employment and Training Service U.S. Department of Labor 800 Capitol Mall, Room W1142 P.O. Box 826880 Sacramento, CA 94280-0001	**California** Phone: (559) 445-5195 Fax: (559) 445-5196 Veterans' Employment and Training Service U.S. Department of Labor 2555 S. Elm Avenue Fresno, CA 93706
California Veterans' Employment and Training Service U.S. Department of Labor 4071 Port Chicago Highway, Suite 250 Concord, CA 94520 Phone: (707) 863-3583 Fax: (707) 864-3489	**California** Veterans' Employment and Training Service U.S. Department of Labor 320 Campus Lane Fairfield, CA 94534 ADVET **David Poulin** poulin.david@dol.gov Phone: (310) 574-6473 Fax: (310) 574-6496	**California** Veterans' Employment and Training Service U.S. Department of Labor 13160 Mindanao Way, Suite 105 Marina del Rey, CA 90292-7904 ADVET **Nancy Ise** ise.Nancy@dol.gov Phone: (714) 687-4845 Fax: (714) 518-2391

California Veterans' Employment and Training Service U.S. Department of Labor 2450 E. Lincoln Avenue Anaheim, CA 92806-4175 ADVET **Joseph D. Moran** moran.joseph@dol.gov Phone: (760) 639-3761 Fax: (760)639-3892	**California** ADVET **Joseph D. Moran** moran.joseph@dol.gov Phone: (760) 639-3761 Fax: (760)639-3892 Veterans' Employment and Training Service U.S. Department of Labor 1949 Avenida del Oro, Ste 114 Oceanside, CA 92056	**California** Phone: (323) 307-0530 Fax: (323) 307-0594 Veterans' Employment and Training Service U.S. Department of Labor 1000 Corporate Center Dr., Suite 550 Monterey Park, CA 91754
Hawaii/Guam DVET **Ann M. Greenlee** greenlee.ann.m@dol.gov Phone: (808) 522-8216 Fax: (808) 586-9258 Veterans' Employment and Training Service U.S. Department of Labor 830 Punchbowl Street, Rm. 315 Honolulu, Hawaii 96813	**Idaho** DVET **Karla Draper** Draper.Karla@dol.gov Phone: (208) 332-8946 Veterans' Employment and Training Service U.S. Department of Labor 317 W. Main Street, Boise, Idaho 83702 Fax: (208) 334-6389	**Nevada** DVET **Darrol L. Brown** brown.darrol@dol.gov Phone: (775) 687-4632 Veterans' Employment and Training Service U.S. Department of Labor 59 East Winnie Lane Carson City, NV 89706 Fax: (775) 687-3976
Nevada ADVET **Doreen A. Owens** owens.doreen.a@dol.gov Phone: (702) 486-2883 Veterans' Employment and Training Service U.S. Department of Labor 1820 E. Sahara Ave, Suite 301 Las Vegas, NV 89104 Fax: (702) 486-2807	**Oregon** Phone: (503) 947-1490 Fax: (503) 947-1492 Veterans' Employment and Training Service U.S. Department of Labor Employment Division Building 875 Union Street, N.E., Room 303 Salem, OR 97311	**Oregon** Veterans' Employment and Training Service U.S. Department of Labor 7795 SW Mohawk Street Tualatin, OR 97062 Phone: (503) 612-4328
Washington Phone: (360) 570-6976 Fax: (360) 570-6978 U.S. Department of Labor Veterans Employment and Training Service P.O. Box 13139 Olympia, WA 98508		

Appendix K

Location of Office of Federal Contract Compliance Programs (OFCCP)

The OFCCP and EEOC have dual jurisdiction. You may file a complaint with the OFCCP if an agency or company has government contracts worth $10,000 or more. Such places include sheriff's departments, police departments, probation and parole office, etc. It is best to bring a class complaint to the OFCCP—two or more persons. For purposes of your veteran's preference, this does not apply. However, OFCCP does have jurisdiction over your disability rights. For example, if you believe you were not hired because of a disability, then OFCCP has jurisdiction over the Rehabilitation Act section 503.

OFFICE OF FEDERAL CONTRACT COMPLIANCE PROGRAMS (OFCCP)

OFCCP Nationwide Office Directory Note: Some states may not have an office but another state may hold jurisdiction over your state.

Alabama	Alaska	Arizona
Birmingham District Office Dept. of Labor OFCCP Medical Forum Building Suite 660 950 22nd Street North Birmingham, AL 35203 Phone: (205) 731-0820 Fax: (205) 731-3466	See Seattle, WA	Phoenix Area Office Dept. of Labor OFCCP 230 North First Avenue, Room 503 Phoenix, AZ 85003 Phone: 602) 514-7033 Fax: (602) 514-7073

Arkansas See Dallas, TX	**Los Angeles District Office** US Dept. of Labor OFCCP 11000 Wilshire Blvd, Suite 8103 Los Angeles, CA 90024 Phone: (310) 235-6800 Fax: (310) 235-6833	**Great San Francisco Bay District Office** US Dept. of Labor OFCCP 90 7th Street, Suite # 11-100 San Francisco, CA 94103 Phone: (415) 625-7828 Fax: (415) 625-7844
San Diego District Office Dept. of Labor OFCCP 550 West C Street, Suite 900 San Diego, CA 92101 Phone: (619) 557-7400 Fax: (619) 557-7490	**San Jose District Office** Dept. of Labor OFCCP 60 South Market St., Suite 410 San Jose, CA 95113 Phone: (408) 291-7384 Fax: (408) 291-7559	**Orange Area Office** Dept. of Labor OFCCP 770 The City Drive, Suite 5700 Orange, CA 92868 Phone: (714) 621-1631 Fax: (714) 621-1640
Colorado Denver District Office Dept. of Labor OFCCP 1999 Broadway, Suite #2205 Denver, CO 80202 Phone: (720) 264-3200 Fax: (720) 264-3211	**Connecticut** Hartford District Office Dept. of LaborOFCCP Wm. R. Cotter Federal Bldg. 135 High Street, Room 219 Hartford, CT 06103-1111 Phone: (860) 240-4277 Fax: (860) 240-4280	**District of Columbia** See Baltimore District Office
Florida Jacksonville Area Office Dept. of Labor OFCCP Charles E. Bennett Federal Building 400 W. Bay Street, Rm 939 Jacksonville, FL 32202 Phone: (904)351-0551 Fax: (904) 351-0560	**Miami Area Office** Dept. of Labor OFCCP 909 SE 1st Avenue, Room 722 Miami, FL 33131 Phone: (305) 536-5670 Fax: (305) 536-5675	**Orlando District Office** Dept. of Labor OFCCP Enterprise Bldg., Suite 100 1001 Executive Center Drive Orlando, FL 32803 Phone: (407) 648-6181 Fax: (407) 648-6084
Georgia Atlanta District Office US Dept. of Labor OFCCP 61 Forsyth Street, SW Room 7B65 Atlanta, GA 30303 Phone: (404) 893-4575 Fax: (404) 893-4576	**Guam** See Honolulu, HI	**Hawaii** *Also serving Guam, American Samoa, and the Northern Marianas Islands* Honolulu Area Office Dept. of Labor OFCCP 300 AlaMoana Blvd Room 7326 MA: Post Office Box 50149 Honolulu, HI 96850 Phone: (808) 541-2933 Fax: (808) 541-2904

Idaho	Illinois	Indiana
See Portland, OR	Chicago District Office US Dept. of Labor OFCCP 230 S. Dearborn Street Room 434 Chicago, IL 60604 Phone: (312) 596-7045 Fax: (312) 596-7085	Indianapolis District Office US Dept. of Labor OFCCP Birch Bayh Federal Building 46 East Ohio Street, Suite 419 Indianapolis, IN 46204 Phone: (317) 226-5860 Fax: (317) 266-5878
Kentucky Louisville Area Office Dept. of Labor OFCCP Gene Snyder U.S. Courthouse & Custom House 601 W. Broadway Rm 15 Louisville, KY 40202-2239 Phone: (502) 582-6275 Fax: (502) 582-6182 Louisville, KY 40202-2239 Phone: (502) 582-6275	**Louisiana** New Orleans District Office US Dept. of Labor OFCCP 600 S. Maestri Place Room 830A New Orleans, LA 70130 Phone: (504) 589-6575 Fax: (504) 589-6064	**Maine** See Boston, MA
Maryland Baltimore District Office US Dept. of Labor OFCCP Appraisers Stores Building 103 South Gay Street Room 202 Baltimore, MD 21202 Phone: (410) 962-6480 Fax: (410) 962-6481	**Massachusetts** Boston District Office US Dept. of Labor OFCCP John F. Kennedy Federal Building Room E-235 Boston, MA 02203 Phone: (617) 624-6780 Fax: (617) 624-6702	**Michigan** Detroit District Office US Dept. of Labor OFCCP 211 West Fort Street Room 1320 Detroit, MI 48226 Phone: (313) 442-3360 Fax: (313) 226-3254
Grand Rapids Area Office US Dept. of Labor OFCCP 50 Louis St., Northwest Suite 300-HUD 2nd Floor, NW-c/o Grand Rapids, MI 49503 Phone: (616) 456-2144 Fax: (616) 456-2197	**Minnesota** Minneapolis Area Office US Dept. of Labor OFCCP Fax: (612) 370-3178 900 2nd Avenue South Suite 480 Minneapolis, MN 55402-3386 Note: Mail is being received at our Milwaukee District Office Phone: (612) 370-3177 Fax: (612) 370-3178	**Mississippi** Jackson Area Office US Dept. of Labor OFCCP McCoy Federal Building 100 West Capitol Street Medical Suite 721 Jackson, MS 39269-1607 Phone: (601) 965-4668 Fax: (601) 965-4726

Missouri	St. Louis District Office	Kansas
Kansas City District Office Dept. of Labor OFCCP Two Pershing Square Building 2300 Main, Suite 1030 Kansas City, MO 64108 Phone: (816) 502-0370 Fax: (816) 426-3888	Dept. of Labor OFCCP Robert A. Young Building 1222 Spruce Street Room 10.207 St. Louis, MO 63103 Phone: (314) 539-6394 Fax: (314) 539-6399	See Chicago, IL
Montana See Dallas, TX	**Nebraska** Omaha District Office Dept. of Labor OFCCP Central Park Plaza 222 S. 15th Street Ste 504B Omaha, NE 68102 Phone: (402) 221-3381 Fax: (402) 221-3379	**Nevada** See Los Angeles, CA
New Hampshire See Boston, MA	**New Jersey** Mountainside District Office US Dept. of Labor OFCCP 200 Sheffield Street, Room 102 Mountainside, NJ 07092 Phone: (908) 317-6969 Fax: (908) 317-6962	**New Mexico** Albuquerque Area Office Dept. of Labor OFCCP 500 Gold Avenue, SW Rm 12000 Albuquerque, NM 87102 Phone: (505) 248-6292 Fax: (505) 245-2132
New York Buffalo Area Office US Dept. of Labor OFCCP	**Niagara Center** 130 South Elmwood Ave Room 536 Buffalo, NY 14202 Phone: (716) 842-2979 Fax: (716) 842-2980	**New York District Office** US Dept. of Labor OFCCP 26 Federal Plaza, Room 36-116 New York, NY 10278 Phone: (212) 264-7743 Fax: (212) 264-8166

North Carolina	**Raleigh Area Office**	**North Dakota**
Charlotte District Office	US Dept. of Labor	See Dallas, TX
US Dept. of Labor	OFCCP	
OFCCP	4407 Bland Road	
Whitehall Corporate	Suite 270	
Center I	Raleigh, NC 27609	
3800 Arco Corporate Drive	Raleigh, NC 27609	
Suite 465	Phone: (919) 790-8248	
Charlotte, NC 28273	Fax: (919) 790-8297	
Phone: (704) 749-3380		
Fax: (704) 749-3381		
Ohio	**Oklahoma**	**Oregon**
Columbus District Office	See Dallas, TX	Portland Area Office
US Dept. of Labor		US Dept. of Labor
OFCCP		OFCCP
John Bricker Federal		620 SW Main Street
Building		Suite 411
200 North High Street		Portland, OR 97201
Room 409		Phone: (503) 326-4112
Columbus, OH 43215		Fax: (503) 326-5746
Phone: (614) 469-5831		
Fax: (614) 469-6606		
Pennsylvania	**Pittsburgh District Office**	**Puerto Rico**
Philadelphia District Office	US Dept. of Labor	Caribbean Field Station
US Dept. of Labor	OFCCP	US Dept. of Labor
OFCCP	Federal Building	OFCCP
Robert N.C. Nix Sr. Fed.	1000 Liberty Ave., Room 2103	525 Franklin D. Roosevelt
Bldg.	Pittsburgh, PA 15222	Avenue
9th & Market Streets,	Phone: (412) 395-6330	Plaza Las Americas, Suite
Rm. 311	Fax: (412) 395-5408	1202
Philadelphia, PA 19107		San Juan, PR 00918
Phone: (215) 597-4122		Phone: (212) 264-7743
Fax: (215) 597-9447		Fax: (212) 264-8166
Rhode Island	South Carolina	**South Dakota**
See Boston, MA	Columbia Area Office	See Dallas, TX
	US Dept. of Labor	
	OFCCP	
	Federal Building	
	1835 Assembly Street, Room 608	
	Columbia, SC 29201	
	Phone: (803) 765-5244	
	Fax: (803) 253-3101	

Tennessee	Memphis Area Office	Texas
Nashville District Office US Dept. of Labor OFCCP 1321 Murfreesboro Road Suite 301 Nashville, TN 37217 Phone: (615) 781-5395 Fax: (615) 781-5399	US Dept. of Labor OFCCP Federal Office Building 167 North Main Street, Suite 101 Memphis, TN 38103 Phone: (901) 544-3458 Fax: (901) 544-4259	Dallas District Office US Dept. of Labor OFCCP 525 S. Griffin Street Room 512 Dallas, TX 75202 Phone: (972) 850-2650 Fax: (972) 850-2651
Houston District Office US Dept. of Labor OFCCP 2320 La Branch, Room 1103 Houston, TX 77004 Phone: (713) 718-3800 Fax: (713) 718-3818	**San Antonio District Office** US Dept. of Labor OFCCP 800 Dolorosa Street Suite 200 San Antonio, TX 78207 Phone: (210) 472-5835 Fax: (210) 472-5842	**Utah** See Dallas, TX
Vermont See Hartford, CT	**Virginia** Also See Washington Metropolitan District Office	**Richmond District Office** US Dept. of Labor OFCCP 400 North 8th Street Room 552 Richmond, VA 23219 Phone: (804) 888-6714 Fax: (804) 888-6715
Virgin Islands See San Juan, PR	**Washington** Seattle District Office US Dept. of Labor OFCCP 1111 Third Avenue, Suite 745 Seattle, WA 98101-3212 Phone: (206) 398-8022 Fax: (206) 398-8010	**West Virginia** See Pittsburgh, PA

Wisconsin	Wyoming	
Milwaukee District Office US Dept. of Labor OFCCP Reuss Federal Building, Suite 1115 310 West Wisconsin Avenue Milwaukee, WI 53203 Phone: (414) 297-3821 Fax: (414) 297-4038	See Dallas, TX	

Appendix L

> On federal resumes, always include dates of employment, hours worked per week for each position, salary, and the names of supervisors. I have seen resumes rejected because the veteran failed to include the number of hours worked per week.

John Smith

P.O. Box 15666

13750 Calumet Rd. Alaska, 99999

Home Phone: (555) 555-5555 •unitedstatemarines22@gmail.com

Key Achievements

- Recognized in having strong skills in problem solving and conflict resolution
- Received leadership commendation from base commanding general
- Recommended to Officer Cadet Training Academy by commanding general
- Promoted early to each next pay grade in US Marine Corps
- Recognized for leadership in conflict resolution as Marine Corps supervisor
- Nominated and received advanced professional leadership training

Education

American Intercontinental University, Hoffman Estates, Illinois

2004, Masters of Business Administration

Park University, Parkville, Missouri

2001, B.S in Criminal Justice Administration, Law Enforcement

Mitchell Community College, North Carolina

Peace Officers Standards and Training (POST) Certification

Specialized Training and Education

- Contemporary Project Management
- Legal Aspects of Business Decisions
- Criminal Investigations

Professional Experience

Federal Law Enforcement Officer, US Department of Justice,

Federal Bureau of Prisons—

741-925 Access Rd. A-25

Washington, D.C 96113

June 2008 to March 2012

Rank: GS-1701-11 (Full Time)

40 hours per week

Supervisor: Joey Wright (retired)/555-555-5555

Salary: $56,000 (approximate)

- Responsible for reviewing contracts for educational material and analyzing the needs and concern for policy and procedure development for the education department. Determined potential problems and opportunity within education services. Analyzed patterns and trends and documented research and surveys to determine technical and functional design for at risk offenders. Possess strong skills in problem solving and conflict resolution in which I first developed in the US Marine Corps as a leader of Marines. Served as Program Coordinator for annual program statement Regional evaluations. Served as Program Coordinator for General Curriculum program from June 2008 to March 2012. Received exceptional performance rating for annual Regional Program Statement evaluation. Responsible for communicating findings to senior level management of program statements evaluations. Advised inmates on laws, rules and regulations of education policy, procedures and protocol. Developed proposals for educational plans for inmate curriculum, and on-the-job training. Exercised technical and administrative supervision of policy and procedure, including performing budget analyst for departmental needs and analyzing cost. Advised and assisted Senior Executive Service members in planning and developing strategies relating to financial management of educational services, training, and equipment procurement.

- **Other Duties**: Served as EEO Liaison for Education Department (3 years). Participated in Employee Relations Program, in-depth knowledge of Federal Labor Relation Act, counseled employees on rights and responsibilities, provided EEO counseling, made recommendation to mid-and senior-level executives on performance improvement plans for employees counseled, coordinated grievances and unfair labor practices charges through union representatives, and responded to correspondence.
- **Awards Received**: Special Acts Award, Time-Off Award.

Detention Educator, Juan County Juvenile Justice Center, Dade, Florida
1410 E. Diversion Damn
Dade, Florida 99999
August 2006 to June 2008
Rank: Teacher (Full Time)
40 hours per week
Supervisor: Bobby Night, Director of Education /555-555-5555
Salary: $56,000 (approximate)

- Provided state-required education curriculum and training to detained youth. Conducted training on skills to overcome youth problems and other cultural and community preconceptions to help cope with problems.

Responsible for explaining laws, rules, and regulation on hiring laws and procedures to assist youth in successfully obtaining employment.

- Recognized for successfully overseeing daily activities of youth and ensuring department policies and procedures are followed.

- Improved educational curriculum and lesson plans, ensure teaching is in accordance with U.S. Department of Education guidelines. Administer screening tools to determine grade levels. Develop policies and procedures for staff and detainees to ensure a positive work environment.

Probation Officer, Dade County Adult Probation, Florida
971 Two Creeks Circle
Miami, Florida 99999
April 2005 to March 2006
Rank: Probation Officer (Full Time)
40 hours per week
Supervisor: Willie Mind, retired /555-555-5555
Salary: $38,000 (approximate)

- Strong problem solving and conflict resolution skills. Excellent skills in investigative fact finding and preparing detailed court reports. Supervised 120 high-, medium-, and low-level criminal offenders. Developed plans for each individual and interpreted and analyzed different policies and programs to determine appropriate use and successful completion of probation. Planned and performed surveys and analyzed self-evaluations of offenders to determine program treatments based on community resources. Ensured timely reporting of each person supervised. Conducted individual and group counseling sessions for adult probationers. Provided expert advice on re-entering the civilian community and presented tools to overcome employment barriers.

- Prepared notices to victims on victim's rights and responsibility.

- Performed criminal investigations and pre-sentence investigations to evaluate probationer's progress.

- Completed searches; made arrests, and reviewed and evaluated criminal records, police reports, and psychiatric/psychological reports.

- In charge of casework on behalf of probationers at the direction of the Superior Court judge.

- Made recommendations on sentencing, disposition, and treatment plans.

- Testified in court, describing investigative results, providing assessment of individual interviews and counseling sessions.

Training and Education Officer/Correctional Officer II, Alaska State Prison Complex-
Tucson/Special Management Unit, San Juan, Alaska
San Juan, Alaska 99999
August 2003 to March 2005
Rank: Training & Education Officer/Correctional Officer II Officer (Full Time)
40 hours per week
Supervisor: Sgt. Modern, retired /555-555-5555
Salary: $28,000 (approximate)

- Responsible for providing updates and recommendations for institutional program statements for inmate programs. Provided instruction, education, and annual training needs of correctional staff. Planned, developed, and implemented training curricula for correctional staff. Evaluated training needs for different institutions and implemented according to institutional needs. Conducted surveys of staff to determine training needs. Provided supervision of death row, security threat groups, and other inmates in the segregation process of denouncing gang membership and general population inmates housed in a level-five unit.

• Assured inmates adhered to department orders and directors instructions through the appropriate application of post orders and good correctional practices.

United States Marine Corps, Active Duty Service
Twenty Nine Palms, California
Rank: Sergeant (E-5) (Full Time)
40 hours per week
Supervisor: Sgt. Dan White (retired) /000-000-000
Salary: $28,000 (approximate)
August 1994 to May 1996 and February 1999 to January 2002

• Numerous assignments: Electrician /Human Resource Specialist (Generalist)

• Provided direct senior leadership for over eighty Marines and civilians in a Marine unit

• Separate functions. Coordinated, planned, and organized numerous projects related to operational readiness and training. Developed strong skills in principles of employee relations and development.

• As a senior leader of Marines, advised commanding officer and senior enlisted personnel on employee relations, training needs, and development. Developed screening checklist and streamlined procedures for endorsements on administrative packages for battalion level signatures. This reduced the processing time, identified errors, and ensured administratively accurate and complete packages were submitted for signature.

- Responsible for evaluating and making recommendations for performance improvement plans.

- Maintained unit-and company-level budget fiscal oversight to include obligated funds, execute purchases, training sessions, and creation and implementation a standards of operating procedures for the budget. Software applications used and required for this task included Standard Accounting, Budget and Reporting System, Wide Area Work Flow, Purchase Request Builder, CitiDirectCard Management System, and the Defense Travel System. Coordinated and supervised the fair distribution of numerous personnel tasking in support of reoccurring and special events in the high visibility events of Marine General and with members of Congress, the base 4th of July picnic, and different Congressional Caucus events.

- Section head safety chief. Created standards of operating procedures and handled the logistical requirements needed to coordinate operational readiness maneuver. Directly responsible for establishing transportation during a convoy move from Camp Pendelton, California, to Twenty-Nine Palms, California.

- Solutions driven professional, advised all levels of management on matters relating to human capital development, leadership, protocol, administrative actions, policy analysis and development, travel, mentoring, morale, welfare, training, and discipline. Developed and managed multiple leadership and training programs. Lead and supervised Marines and sailors and managed work flow, ensuring timely and effective execution of administrative, logistical, and operational functions. Possessed superior communication and problem-solving skills.